Philosophical Foundations of Leadership

Philosophical Foundations of Leadership

David Cawthon

With an introduction by Blue Clark

LONDON AND NEW YORK

First published 2002 by Transaction Publishers

Published 2017 by Routledge
2 Park Square, Milton Park, Abingdon, Oxon OX14 4RN
711 Third Avenue, New York, NY 10017, USA

Routledge is an imprint of the Taylor & Francis Group, an informa business

Library of Congress Catalog Number: 2002072136

Library of Congress Cataloging-in-Publication Data

Cawthon, David.
    Philosophical foundations of leadership / David Cawthon ; with an introduction by Blue Clark.
        p. cm.
    Includes bibliographical references and index.
    ISBN 0-7658-0125-6 (alk. paper)
        1. Leadership—Philosophy. I. Title.

HM1261 .C39 2002
303.3'4'01—dc21   2002072136

ISBN 13: 978-0-7658-0125-8 (hbk)

Contents

Introduction

Blue Clark

The book you are about to read is about leadership, with examples drawn from thinkers ranging from ancient to modern times. But before the book is introduced to the reader some prefatory remarks about the late author are in order.

David Lee Cawthon (1938-2001) wrote a well-received series of articles examining how great thinkers dealt with the challenges of leadership. Angus MacDonald, publisher of the *St. Croix Review*, is to be thanked for his perceptive grasp of the importance of the series that he first printed and for his guidance in seeking a book publisher for it.

Dave Cawthon's pursuit of the topic extended throughout his lifetime. However, the series arose from another work that served as a catalyst. Like so many teachers, I read lists of books in the same way gardeners examine flower catalogues. One day my eye fell on the citation for James O'Toole's *The Executive's Compass* (1993), as well as a brief description of its contents. The sketch intrigued me. Instinctively, I knew this was a title that would also intrigue Dave. He would be interested in O'Toole's value compass and the book's ethical discussions. I ordered the book, received it, and after thumbing its pages to confirm my earlier assumption, I left it with a note for Dave. After some time elapsed, he contacted me with an enthusiastic response to the work. The gestation process for his own project had begun. Still later, Dave participated in the wide-ranging discussions held as a part of the summertime Aspen Institute, where O'Toole for years had been moderator of the Institute's Executive Seminars. Those exchanges stimulated Dave's thinking, further fueling his desire to undertake his own study of leadership. In addition, I continually nipped at Dave's heels about his writing project.

In the meantime Dave's work continued to intrude into his thinking, writing, and golfing time. Dave saw university service in a wide variety of leadership roles on more than one campus. Whether a school dean or an academic vice president, he worked to heal rifts whether among faculty, trustees, or students. In 1997 he became the interim president of Oklahoma City University. Those were tough times that tested his abilities to the fullest. He preserved the institution in the face of multiple threats. As a result of working closely with him through the challenges I came to admire Dave greatly. He displayed all of the qualities of an able leader. Moreover, he led with aplomb. And, he kept one eye focused on the long-term religious consequences that actions have on the human soul.

David Cawthorn kept the religious element of human existence in the forefront of his life and of his thinking. He occupied the T. K. Hendrick Chair of Management within the Meinders Business School where he was an exceptionally capable teacher. He also had extensive instruction experience overseas. His teaching focused on organizational behavior and leadership. Students would comment that his class had transformed their lives and how his teaching and exhortations had placed them on a productive path for the future. He was among the finest teachers on a campus well known for its teaching. In his classroom as in his life, he exuded a devotion to religious-based learning.

The combination of religious focus and concern for questions of leadership led him to assess how great thinkers in the past had dealt with similar issues. In his series of articles for the *St. Croix Review,* Dave examined Aristotle, Rousseau, Hegel, Marx, and prelates such as Aquinas as they struggled with vexing questions of what makes a successful leader.

Lung cancer quietly assaulted Dave during his final year. He underwent a successful course of treatment during that time only to succumb quickly at the end to congestive heart failure. Again, his sustaining faith served as an example to all of us who knew him of how to face the inevitable end.

He left many legacies, centered on words like family, church, friends, and students. Among his publications, he left the series of articles that became this book. The work is a testament to Dave Cawthon's wide-ranging thinking, so often focused on leadership. Often, he would deftly swing a dinner table conversation toward a discussion of a recent news topic dealing with some aspect of leadership, then steer the comments in the direction of a more in-depth examination of the qualities that make a leader.

Dave's book comes at an opportune time because religion, in all aspects of life and work, is the subject of increasing attention. Commentators, media programming, and printed works address, and reappraise, religious issues in societies. As David Cawthon frequently noted, leadership never goes out of style as a topic. Questions of what constitutes leadership and leaders are ever present in a republic. At some point all of us either hurl a plaudit or a barb at our leaders.

A book triggered Dave Cawthon's thinking to focus on leadership. He would be most well served if his own book stirred a similar response from readers. Through these pages the individual will discern how engaging and compelling Dave was as a person and teacher. His queries into the nature of leadership are relevant today, and likely will remain so in the future.

1

Leadership and the Coding of Our Souls

"No two people are born exactly alike...there are innate differences which fit them for different occupations."—Plato

Several years ago one of this century's foremost scholars on leadership suggested that there is an unconscious conspiracy that prevents leaders from emerging in our society. "Circumstances conspire against them," Warren Bennis explains in his book, *Why Leaders Can't Lead.* "And so—without meaning to—do the American people."[1] As he developed his thesis, he pointed to an array of complexities that stand as obstacles to effective leadership. Notable among them was a commitment to the status quo, a preoccupation with individual rights, selfishness of the "Me Decade," an unwillingness to cooperate with neighbors, and feelings of helplessness among followers. "People float, but they don't dream," Bennis writes. "And people without a dream are less easily inspired by a leader's vision."[2]

Perhaps his indictment is true. Many leaders would agree that if it were not for such an unconscious conspiracy in our society, they could be more effective. On the other hand, I would suggest that if we would examine our methodologies as we attempt to understand the complexities of leadership, we would find them to be somewhat limited. Although Bennis' analysis describes rather accurately those obstacles with which leaders must contend, like most discussion regarding this topic today, it fails to address the philosophical underpinnings of leadership itself. It focuses on circumstance. As a result, it fails to address the nature of humans, and, accordingly, the unique talents of those who would lead. It fails to consider a most important reason as to why some leaders can't lead: *they simply don't have it in them.* Or, as researchers Shelly Kirkpatrick and Edwin Locke have observed, they don't have the *right stuff.*[3] Such a proposition, how-

5

ever, is not contemporary in origin. Instead, it is rooted in the teachings of Plato, and it is upon his shoulders that we stand when we
contend that leaders can't lead because they were not *born* to lead.
Simply stated, leadership is not inherent within the codes of their
souls.

Indeed, Plato would find our approaches toward understanding
leadership to be rather amusing, for they do not address those philosophical considerations necessary for meaningful answers to our
questions. They do not examine the nature of man. *Who should lead?*
What gives one the right to exact obedience from others? These are
the questions that Plato would ask, and until we answer them, he
would argue, we will fail in our attempts to understand the nature of
leadership. Certainly, Plato addressed such questions, but we cannot appreciate his answers without an understanding of his philosophy regarding the nature of man, without an understanding of what
it means to be human.

Philosophically, Plato was an idealist. He taught that what we perceive through our senses are only shadows, finite imitations of the
ideal, but not the ideal itself. Professor S. E. Frost, Jr. explains as
follows:

> For Plato, the world which we see, touch, and experience through our other senses is
> not real, but is a copy world. In it we find things changing, coming and going, and in
> great abundance. It is a world of many mistakes, deformities, evils. It exists and we
> experience it every day. But it is not real.
>
> There is, however, a real world in which are to be found the true things of which all
> that we experience are mere copies. He called this the world of 'ideas.' Here is to be
> found the ideal tree of which all trees which we see are copies, the ideal house, and ideas
> of all other objects in the universe. These are perfect, do not change in any way, never
> fade or die, but remain forever.
>
> The 'ideas' or 'forms'. . . were never created, but have existed from the very
> beginning in just the perfect state in which they will always exist. They are independent
> of all things, and are not influenced by the changes that take place in the world which we
> experience through our senses. These objects which we experience are reflections of
> these 'external patterns.'[4]

For Plato, the *ideal* is eternal; it is divine. And the *ideal* resides in
each of us, imprisoned by our bodies. Such is the nature of man, and
it is our human task to open ourselves to those transcendental ideas
that lie within us. It is our task to seek unity between the natural and
the supernatural, between the physical and the metaphysical.

Unfortunately, according to Plato, only a few have the inherent
ability to distinguish between the *real* and the *ideal*, to see beyond

the shadows. Most of us are confused. We are blind to the *ideal*. We are held bondage by the shadows of imperfection within our world, and we need others to help release us from our imprisonment. We need others to direct us toward goodness, and truth, and beauty. And those who would do so are our leaders. They are our guardians. They are our *philosopher kings*. In his book, *The Passion of the Western Mind*, Richard Taurus summarizes Plato's allegory of the cave to illustrate this bondage:

> Human beings are like prisoners chained to the wall of a dark subterranean cave, where they can never turn around to see the light of a fire that is higher up at a distance behind them. When objects outside the cave pass in front of the light, the prisoners mistake as real what are merely shadows created on the wall. Only one who is freed from his chains and leaves the cave to enter into the world beyond can glimpse true reality, though when first exposed to the light he may be so overwhelmed by its dazzling luminosity as to be unable to recognize its actual character. Yet once he habituates himself to the light and comes to recognize the true causes of things, he would hold precious the clarity of his new understanding.[5]

Without question, those who have been freed from the shadows of the cave, that is, our leaders, are inherently different from those who remain in darkness. Although each of us shares the same essence, that is, humanness, Plato teaches that our individual souls are not the same.

First, some have souls coded toward the realm of the *appetitive*. Driven by their physical appetites, they base their lives on the pursuit of physical pleasure. They seek passion; they seek luxury; they measure success in terms of the accumulation of wealth and trinkets. The more *spirited* souls among us are warriors. They seek power, striving for victory, regardless of the battlefield. Finally, those with more *rational* souls delight in the acquisition of knowledge. They are not victims of lust and physical pleasure. Their goodness sets them apart from those who are self-serving, for they seek only wisdom and understanding. Theirs is the life of the mind, not encumbered by the impoverishment of material gain and power as they seek union with that which is eternal. Such, then, are the codes of our individual souls. According to Plato, providence gives each of us different talents and abilities. "No two people are born exactly alike," he writes. "There are innate differences which fit them for different occupations."[6]

From this premise Plato derives his understanding of the nature of our organizations as well as the inherent roles of our leaders. The ideal society, he explains, should reflect the nature of its citizens. It should have the same three distinct components. The *appetitive* component would consist of craftsmen and artisans, those who seek the material rewards of life, those who seek pleasure, those whose lives are driven by passion rather than reason. The *spirited* component would be the defenders of our society, soldiers and warriors, the physically strong, those who would courageously protect us from our enemies. The *rational* component would include those committed to understanding and knowledge, those with vision of the higher good, those able to distinguish between shadow and light. These, Plato writes, are the guardians of our society. These are our *philosopher-kings*. These are our corporate managers, our political leaders, our religious prelates, our military generals. Leadership is their talent. It is deeply embedded within the code of their souls.

At the same time, Plato teaches that providence has appropriated talents to each of us in a manner most consistent with the needs of our society. It needs musicians. It needs shoemakers. It needs craftsmen. It needs physicians. Consequently, each of us must understand *who we are* in terms of the codes of our individual souls. If we have been assigned the soul of an engineer, for example, we should develop that talent to the greatest extent possible. In brief, Plato would agree with twentieth-century philosopher Joseph Campbell. Each of us must discover our individual *bliss*, our dominant talent, the code of our soul if we are to find meaning and happiness in our lives. Doing otherwise brings misery to ourselves. More important, doing otherwise brings imbalance and deprivation to the society in which we live.

Unlike many of our current approaches to education in the United States, however, young people in Plato's *Republic* were not left to their own devices to discover their unique abilities. Nor were their parents charged with such an important and critical responsibility. This activity was the ultimate responsibility of the philosopher-kings. All children were raised and educated by the guardians of the state until they reached adulthood. Only after a long evaluation process had been completed would the code of a child's soul be identified. Once identified, each would be directed toward those professions most appropriate to his individual talents. Equally important, each would develop her unique abilities for the rest of her life.

Certainly, Plato believed that only a few among us have been given the talent of leadership, and the corresponding responsibility related to such talent is overwhelming. By any standard we might imagine, it is awesome. Those whose souls were identified to be coded for leadership, were isolated for intense preparation, primarily in philosophy, mathematics, music, and those intellectual disciplines that bring order to the mind. They were required to excel in their pursuit of goodness, not only for themselves, but for all within society. Virtue and selflessness were at the core of their training, for Plato viewed leaders much as he viewed physicians. Physicians were not to be trained to pursue self-serving needs. They were not to be concerned with material gain. Instead, they were taught to act only on behalf of the patient's good, and, in the *Republic*, the patient understood who, between the two of them, was the expert.

Accordingly, Plato teaches that leaders should provide vision and understanding for their followers. They must not be self-serving; they must not be driven by physical pleasure; they must not be motivated by wealth. Instead, they must be men and women of virtue. They must seek wisdom and understanding. They must always act on behalf of those whom providence has placed under their rule. "They must have the right sort of intelligence and ability," Plato writes, "they must look upon the commonwealth as their special concern— the sort of concern that is felt for something so closely bound up with oneself that its interests and fortunes, for good or ill, are held identical with one's own."[7]

It is important to note that his teaching regarding one's *right* to lead is not based on an accident of birth. The Divine Right of Kings held no sway with Plato, for to him, leadership is not hereditary. Although he acknowledges differences among humans, he does not suggest, for example, that the heirs of leaders should lead, nor that the children of laborers should be laborers. Instead, he believes that the souls of all should be examined as guardians identify those who are suited for leadership. Plato explains as follows:

[T]he god who fashioned you mixed gold in the composition of those among you who are fit to rule, so that they are of the most precious quality; and he put silver in the Auxiliaries, and iron and brass in the farmers and craftsmen. Now, since you are all of one stock, although your children will generally be like their parents, sometimes a golden parent may have a silver child or a silver parent a golden one, and so on with other combinations. So the first and chief injunction laid by heaven upon the Ruler is that, among all the things of which they must show themselves good guardians, there is none that needs to be so carefully watched as the mixture of metals in the souls of children. If a child of their own is born with an alloy of iron or brass, they must, without the smallest pity, assign him the station proper to his nature and thrust him out among the craftsmen or the farmers. If, on the contrary, these classes produce a child with gold or silver in his composition, they will promote him, according to his value, to be a Guardian or an Auxiliary. They will appeal to a prophecy that ruin will come upon the state when it passes into the keeping of a man of iron or brass.[8]

Regardless, Plato was not chauvinistic. Even though he acknowledges that women are physically weaker than men, he proposes that every occupation should be open to both.[9] It does not matter whether one's soul is composed of gold or silver or iron or brass. Providence does not discriminate on the basis of gender. What does matter, however, is the proper identification and subsequent assignment of the soul. As Plato notes, ruin will come to the state (as well as the organization or the company) that assigns a soul of iron or brass to a leadership position.

In summary, Plato proposed that leadership requires a special talent, and only those few who possess such talent should be trained toward its proper utilization. Having rigorously developed this talent, the philosopher-kings, the guardians, should rule. Not only is it their right, it is their duty. Similarly, those whose souls have been marked for the *appetitive* and the *spirited* functions of life should develop the talents assigned them by providence. It is only when individuals fail to develop and apply their unique abilities that disharmony occurs, for in the divine scheme of things, nature has harmoniously distributed the talent necessary for a society to achieve its perfection. For one to deny his code and pursue a path for which he has not been coded is to commit an injustice against the balance of society. It is to prevent that society from achieving its perfection.[10]

Given this perspective of Plato's teachings regarding the nature of man and society, we can more readily appreciate his answers to our questions regarding leadership. *Who should lead?* For Plato the answer is simple. Those, and *only* those, whose souls have been coded to become leaders. As religious leaders often attribute their leadership role to the will of God, that is, *You have not chosen me, rather I have chosen you*, Plato would assert that one's leadership role has been determined by providence. The souls of the leaders seek justice; they understand the differences between light and shadow; they unselfishly seek good for all within their organizations. Not only *should* they lead, they *must* lead. It is their destiny to do so. And to allow those whose souls have not been coded to lead to assume leadership positions would be to condemn an organization, a business, a state, to ruin and decay. Such, according to Plato, is the nature of things.

Thus, rather than concern himself with an array of external complexities that prevent leaders from being able to lead, Plato explores the meaning of leadership in terms of the codes of people's souls. Rather than concentrate on the external attributes of leadership, he attempts to wrestle with those haunting questions that have plagued humans throughout their history: *What is man? Who should lead? Why?* In terms often used by Stephen Covey, rather than look *outside-in* as he examines the nature of leadership, Plato looks *inside-out*. He doesn't analyze the behaviors of leaders; he seeks to understand their souls. "Who are you?" he would ask. "Why should I follow you?" The external contingencies that permeate our current approach to understanding leadership would have little meaning for him.

Although Plato's writings date back more than two centuries, it seems apparent that many contemporary leaders would readily identify with the teachings of Plato, for his thought has provided a strong foundation upon which we have developed many of our theories regarding leadership. The performance standards of Frederick Taylor, the bureaucracy of Max Weber, the efficiencies of Frank and Lillian Gilbreth, and many of the managerial principles of Henri Fayol bear a strong resemblance to Plato's *Republic*. They center on specialization. Employees are not considered to be of equal ability. They are expected to comply joyfully with the directives of management, the guardians of industry. They should well understand who, between the two of them, is the expert. As Bernard Bass reminds us in his *Handbook of Leadership*, prior to the mid-twentieth century, most of us believed that individuals possess different degrees of intelligence, energy, and moral force, and in whatever direction the masses may be influenced to go, they are always led by the superior few.[11]

Many continue to share that view. And rightly so. Regardless of the leader, whether it be Alexander the Great, or George Washington, or Lee Kuan Yew, or Golda Mier, or Martin Luther King, these superior few strongly influenced the direction of their followers. And it was no accident. In the words of Kirkpatrick and Locke, they had the *right stuff*. In the words of Plato, it was in the *code of their souls*.

Whether they share such views or not, however, few who lead our organizations would openly define themselves as philosopher-kings. In a democracy it would be elitist for one to declare that he or she was *born* to lead. The behavioral sciences have, for the most part, leveled the playing field regarding our understanding of the distribution of talent among humans. The Bell Curve no longer applies. Speaking honestly, however, do not most managers believe that they are different from their employees? Would they not claim to be more talented and knowledgeable than their followers? Would they not suggest that it is this superior ability that gives them their right to lead? Would they not believe that their souls are made of gold, while the souls of their employees are made of silver and brass and iron? Would leaders not agree that their organizations would flounder and fail should power be mistakenly assigned to those whose souls have not been coded for leadership? Certainly, they would. And when they do, they are standing squarely on the shoulders of Plato.

Similarly, women should appreciate the teachings of Plato, for even though he was a European white male and, therefore, the target of scathing attack by the historical and literary revisionists of our societies, he was among the first within Western culture to recognize that leadership is not gender specific. Certainly, Aristotle did not. Nor did most other Greek and Roman philosophers. And although he acknowledged that women, for the most part, lack the physical strength of men, those whose focus is the inequities of male dominance would have little charge against Plato. His concern was with the essence of the soul rather than the reproductive organs of the body.

These are but a few examples as to how our leaders have been influenced by the writings of Plato. There are many others. Unfortunately, for the latter part of the twentieth century we have failed to recognize the important contributions that philosophy can make to our understanding of leadership. We have failed to draw distinctions among all those who have provided us the philosophical foundations of leadership in Western culture. Instead, our bookshelves are lined with behavioral observations that tend to obfuscate rather than enlighten. We can describe leadership, but we lack an understanding of what it is.

Thus, it seems appropriate to redirect our focus and depart from our preoccupation with behaviors and contingencies and unconscious conspiracies. If we are to understand leadership, we must shift our attention away from empirical observations that explain what *leaders do* and begin examining once more those philosophical propositions that tell us *what leaders are*. For then, and only then, will we be able to penetrate the mystery of this most elusive topic. What better place to begin than by reviewing once more *The Republic* of Plato?

Notes

1. Warren Bennis, *Why Leaders Can't Lead* (San Francisco, CA: Jossey-Bass Publishers, 1989), xi.
2. Ibid., xiii.
3. Shelly A. Kirkpatrick and Edwin A. Locke, "Leadership: Do Traits Matter?" *Academy of Management Executive,* 5 (1991) 58.
4. S. E. Frost, Jr., *Teachings of the Great Philosophers* (New York: Doubleday Anchor Books, 1962), 10.
5. Richard Taurus, *The Passion of the Western Mind* (New York: Ballantine Books, 1991), 41-42.
6. Plato, *The Republic of Plato*, trans. F. M. Cornford (New York: Oxford University Press, 1945), 56.
7. Ibid., 104.
8. Ibid., 106-107
9. Ibid., 153.
10. Ibid.,141.
11. Bernard M. Bass, *Bass & Stodgill's Handbook of Leadership,* 3rd ed. (New York: The Free Press, 1990.)

2

Aristotle on Leadership:
Free from the Tyranny of Passion

"[F]rom the hour of their birth, some are marked out for subjection, others for rule."
—*Aristotle*

A stream of scholarship has recently emerged concerning our understanding of leadership in contemporary society. Having been deluged by a myriad of contingency and behavioral theories for the latter part of the twentieth century, a few scholars now seek an alternate approach to this most elusive topic. Rather than continuing to rely on the methodologies of popular psychology, they are turning to philosophy to enhance their understanding of leadership.

An example of this shift in methodology can be found in Tom Morris' book, *If Aristotle Ran General Motors.* Although his book often lacks the intensity of philosophical scrutiny, it, nevertheless, proposes that the study of leadership must be more than a long series of empirical observations.

Morris is correct. It is quite appropriate to seek unity between the physical and the metaphysical, between the natural and the supernatural. Yet, in many ways his work falls short, for it fails to grope with those philosophical questions that should lie at the core of our inquiry. *What does it mean to be human? Are we, indeed, equal? Who among us should lead?* Until we approach these questions, we cannot understand what gives one the right to exact obedience from another. And the answers to these questions are rooted in our philosophies regarding the nature of humanity. Without question, Aristotle has answers to our questions. Yet, before we can assess his answers, we must briefly examine his philosophy regarding the nature of the universe.

Unlike his mentor, Plato, Aristotle was a *realist*. His feet were firmly planted in the world of nature. Although he believed in the existence of the *ideal*, he did not share Plato's contention that the *ideal* exists apart from nature. Instead, Aristotle believed it to be *one* with the matter it informed. What we perceive through our senses *is not* a mere imitation of the real world; *it is the real world itself.*

Yet, the fact of change threatens our understanding of reality. The acorn, for example, will change into a tree. The girl will become a woman. Nothing will remain the same. Thus, the perplexing philosophical question: How can an object be what it is since it exists in a state of continuous change?

In order to explain these changes, Aristotle proposed that matter continuously moves toward its proper end, taking on different forms, becoming what it was intended to become. Included within its *actuality* is the *potential* to become something else. Professor S. E. Frost, Jr. cites the example of a sculptor creating a statue to explain:

> If we wish to understand the universe, then, we may think of it in terms of a sculptor producing a statue. But, while in the case of Plato the sculptor is independent, free from his marble, in the case of Aristotle he is dependent on his marble. His idea of a perfect statue is actually in the marble, a form which the marble seeks to realize.
>
> Therefore, Aristotle taught that every object in the universe had four causes. The first corresponds to the idea of the statue which the artist has before he begins work, the form which is to be realized. This he called the "formal cause." Then there is the marble with which the artist is to work, the matter. This is the "material cause." The third cause is that by which the statue is made, the tools employed to make the statue. This he called the "efficient cause" or "moving cause." The fourth cause is the purpose or end for which the statue is made, that for the sake of which the work is done. This he termed the "final cause."[1]

Aristotle, thus, taught that all phenomena have a purpose, that toward which they strive, and it is from within this framework that he developed his philosophy regarding the nature of humanity. If all things move toward a final cause, he asks, what is the final cause of humans? What is our purpose? Toward what are we striving? Aristotle offers answers to these questions in the first chapter of his *Nicomachean Ethics*. Simply stated, he taught that it is the nature of humans to be happy, and it is toward happiness that each of us strives. Professor Austin Fagothy explains this proposition as follows:

> Happiness is the end of man. It is not inactivity, but action, else one could be happy while asleep. It must be the highest kind of action, not done for something else but desirable for its own sake. It is not amusement, which is only relaxation between work. It is not found in producing things, since such actions are for the sake of the product and

happiness is for its own sake. It is not action of the body or senses, but of what is noblest and best in us, our reason. It is not activity of the practical reason, for this is full of care and trouble; but of the speculative or theoretical reason which acts in quiet and leisure, for we work to have leisure. Hence it is not the activity of the soldier and statesman, but of the sage and scholar.

Because it is the good life, it is the life of virtue, and of the highest virtue; not merely of courage and temperance which fit a man for practical life, but of the intellectual virtues which fit a man for contemplation, the contemplation of the highest truth and good. The contemplative life is most pleasant, leisurely, continuous, enduring, and self-sufficing. This is the life of God and it is the best.[2]

Although Aristotle believed happiness can only be found through the pursuit of virtue, he did not suggest that human emotions and feelings should be denounced and ignored. He was a realist. Nevertheless, he did contend that our passions must be tempered. They must be controlled by the mind. The irrational must be directed by the rational. There must be balance. Accordingly, the *golden mean* became Aristotle's guide for the achievement of excellence. Nothing in excess. Whether our action be toward the moral virtues of courage, temperance, and self-respect, or the intellectual virtues of art, scientific knowledge, practical wisdom, philosophic wisdom, or intuitive reason, excellence lies at the mean. It lies between the extremes.

Appropriate virtuous activity, however, should not be determined as if it were a mathematical calculation, for it is not an objective mean. Instead, the golden mean must be understood relative to the situation in which one finds oneself. It must be reflective and thoughtful. It must be rational. It must lead to realistic action. Thus, the virtuous person is one, who, through deliberation, blends action with knowledge, and, in doing achieves happiness.

Yet, Aristotle did not believe that all humans have the intellectual capacity to participate in the truly happy life, and it is from this framework that he developed his leadership dyad. Basically, he taught that there are two types of human beings. Those whose lives are virtuous and rational, and those whose lives are directed by passion, whim, and social convention. To the former he bestowed citizenship within the community, for they had the ability to enable the community to achieve its purposes. Accordingly, they were assigned roles of leisure in order that they might contemplate and act upon the *ultimate good*. As *freemen*, they were free from the necessities of work.

To the latter, however, he denied citizenship. Instead, they were subjugated to the rule of the *freemen*, for according to Aristotle,

women, laborers, artisans, and farmers lacked the ability to participate in the good life. Driven by lust, gluttony, and physical necessity, they lacked virtue. They lacked the ability as well as the time to
contemplate the *ultimate good.*

In brief, Aristotle was in no way an egalitarian in his delineation
of the leadership dyad. For him, humans are not created equal,
whether by nature or by law. He explains,

> But is there any one thus intended by nature to be a slave, and for whom such a
> condition is expedient and right, or rather is not all slavery a violation of nature?
>   There is no difficulty in answering this question, on grounds both of reason and of
> fact. For that some should rule and others be ruled is a thing not only necessary, but
> expedient; from the hour of their birth, some are marked out for subjection, others for
> rule. . . . Whereas the lower animals cannot even apprehend a principle; they obey their
> instincts. And indeed the use made of slaves and of tame animals is not very different;
> for both with their bodies minister to the needs of life. . . . And, if this is true of the body,
> how much more just that a similar distinction should exist in the soul? But the beauty of
> the body is seen, whereas the beauty of the soul is not seen. It is clear, then, that some
> men are by nature free, and others slaves, and that for these latter slavery is both
> expedient and right.[3]

Accordingly, the *freeman* should rule the slave, for the slave lacks
virtue. Like lower forms of animals, he lacks the capacity to appre-
hend principle. His destiny is to use his body to minister to the needs
of his life. Simply stated, as the soul is superior to the body, so too is
the *freeman* superior to the slave.

For women and children, however, Aristotle's approach to the dyad
is somewhat different. Even though he considers both to be inferior
to the *freeman*, he allows that children have the potential to be virtuous. Moreover, unlike slaves, women have virtues peculiar to their
nature.

> But the kind of rule differs;–the freeman rules over the slave after another manner from
> that in which the male rules over the female, or the man over the child; although the parts
> of the soul are present in all of them, they are present in different degrees. For the slave
> has no deliberative faculty at all; the woman has, but it is without authority, and the child
> has, but it is immature. So it must necessarily be supposed to be with the moral virtues
> also; all should partake of them, but only in such manner and degree as is required by
> each for the fulfillment of his duty. . . . Clearly, then, moral virtue belongs to all of them;
> but the temperance of a man and of a woman, or the courage and justice of a man and of
> a woman, are not, as Socrates maintained, the same; the courage of a man is shown in
> commanding, of a woman in obeying. . . . The child is imperfect, and therefore obvi-
> ously his virtue is not relative to himself alone, but to the perfect man and to his teacher,
> and in like manner the virtue of the slave is relative to a master.[4]

As a result, he taught that since a slave has no deliberative faculty, the master must lead as a despot. Since the child has the potential for virtue, it should be treated as a king would treat his subjects. Since the wife has virtue, though it be without authority, she should participate in the management of the household to the extent her specific nature might allow.

As might be readily surmised, if Aristotle did, indeed, run General Motors, no women would be in the corporate boardroom. There would be no representation of labor on its board of directors. These inner-sancta of power would be the exclusive domain of the more talented, the more virtuous, the more privileged of our society. Women and laborers would be relegated to roles of obedience.

It should be noted, however, that although such distinctions in the leadership dyad have strong elitist implications, Aristotle's leaders were men of courage and temperance. They were learned. They were compassionate. They sought the *ultimate good*, not only for themselves, but for all who were under their rule. They were undaunted by private interest and the pursuit of trinkets. Free from the tyranny of passion, their leadership was rooted in justice and virtue.

Interestingly, Aristotle seems to hedge in his identification of those who should be the leaders within his society of *freemen*. At times he suggests that each, being equal, should take his turn as leader, noting that since no one man among equals is superior to the others, none should have permanent rule. Later in his *Politics*, he proposes that many of the primary talents required by a society may be inherent at various times within the same individual, thus suggesting that citizens should be warriors when they are young, leaders when they reach middle age, and priests as they grow old.

Regardless, like Plato, Aristotle held that there are those who are born to lead; the rest are born to follow. For Plato, however, such leadership endowments were distributed among many throughout society, regardless of one's accident of birth, and it was the responsibility of the philosopher-kings to identify those who possessed these talents and prepare them for their proper place in society. Aristotle, however, taught that *freemen* are mostly born of *free* parents. Thus, citizenship was a birth right. Only those born into the leisure class could be citizens. Likewise, the sons of slaves remained slaves, for as laborers they lacked the time necessary for the leisurely contemplation of the *ultimate good*. Their task was to work. Considering physical labor to be demeaning to the soul, Aristotle believed that slaves were unfit for virtue. Consequently, the sons of slaves were never afforded the opportunity to rise to the status of *freemen*.

In many ways, Aristotle's proposition that leaders should be men of virtue has provided us a philosophical foundation that has served us well. Although we are often disappointed, we denounce self-serving behavior among our leaders. For the most part, we have little tolerance for opportunistic demagogues pursing personal gain at the expense of others. Without question, if Aristotle were to run General Motors, we would find leadership seeking to unify the corporation toward the *ultimate good* common to all humans. We would find trust. We would find truth and honesty. We would find beauty and goodness. We would find focus on those qualities of our souls that separate us from animals.

In other ways, however, it is painful to illustrate how Aristotle's philosophy regarding the inequalities of humans served for more than 2000 years as a foundation for leadership behavior in our society. Without question, such ideas within Western democracies have become mostly abhorrent. But it is important to highlight Aristotle's attempt to wrestle with these issues, for these are the issues that have confronted humans throughout history. Indeed, current examples of our attempts to address them are numerous: affirmative action, civil rights, human rights, women's rights, worker's rights. Each is rooted in concepts of equality. Each is embedded in one's understanding of the nature of humans. And whereas we who live in a democracy may not be satisfied with Aristotle's response to these issues, there is considerable evidence that we are equally dissatisfied with our own responses. Leaders speak of equality; yet, they often treat others as inferior, as the *freeman* would treat his slave. The *haves* often deny human dignity to the *have nots*. Indeed, it is not all that uncommon to find that some continue to proclaim a *natural* superiority over others within our society.

For example, many would deny women opportunities to develop their leadership talents under the guise that such is not within the scope of their intended nature. They would agree with Aristotle's assertion that the courage of a man is properly manifested by his ability to *command*, while the moral virtue of a woman is revealed through her willingness to *obey*. As a result, the *glass ceiling* continues to exist, not only for women but for all considered by some to be innately inferior, either by gender or by race. And wherever we justify elitism based on an accident of birth, whether in our corporate boardrooms or within the hierarchies of our military institutions, or within the sanctuaries of our cathedrals, we are acknowledging our agreement with Aristotle's contention regarding a natural inequality among humans.

Indeed, the history of the United States is filled with examples. Even though our Constitution was framed upon concepts of equality advanced by John Locke, those who helped shape American political thought often stood on the philosophical shoulders of Aristotle as well. In an 1813 letter to John Adams,[5] for example, Thomas Jefferson noted that there is a *natural* aristocracy among men. While refuting the *pseudo-aristoi* position that included the accidents of beauty, wealth, and birth among the five pillars of an aristocracy, Jefferson concluded that the elements of a *natural* aristocracy are simply genius and virtue. Accordingly, he considered these to be the most precious gifts that *nature* has given us. This is not to suggest that Jefferson would deny citizenship to those with lesser ability. He would not. It is, however, to note that Jefferson drew clear distinctions concerning the inequalities of ability and virtue among human kind. He, as did many of our founding fathers, shared Aristotle's convictions regarding women and children and slaves. And, as his biographers continue to remind us, he anguished over those convictions throughout his life.

We should not be surprised, then, to find that throughout history our philosophies regarding the nature of humans have been influenced by Aristotle. We should not be surprised to read of Jim Crow laws. We should not be surprised that until this century women were denied the right to vote because they were considered to be naturally inferior. This is our heritage in Western society, and whenever we proclaim superiority based on race or gender or other accidents of birth, whether it be within our countries or within our organizations, we are witnessing our agreement with Aristotle's teachings of inequality.

Without question, the philosophical insights of Aristotle have made a considerable impact upon our current understanding of leadership. Of all the philosophers who emerged from this golden age of Greek history, along with Socrates and Plato, he is among those who have been most influential in the formation of our understanding of leadership. And rightly so! For Aristotle confronted those difficult issues that continue to haunt us today. And if we are to seek a deeper understanding of what it means to be a leader, we, like Aristotle, must confront those same questions that he posed more than 2,400 years ago. *What is the nature of humans? What is the meaning of equality? What gives one the right to exact obedience from another?*

Notes

1.   S. E. Frost, Jr., *Basic Teachings of the Great Philosophers* (New York: Doubleday Anchor Books, 1962),14.
2.   Austin Fagothy, *Right and Reason* (St. Louis, MO: C. V. Mosby Company, 1955), 43-44.
3.   Aristotle, "Politics," in Richard McKeon, ed., *The Works of Aristotle*, trans. Benjamin Jowett (New York: Random House, 1941), 1131-1133.
4.   Ibid. 1144-1145.
5.   Thomas Jefferson, *Thomas Jefferson: Writings* (New York: The Library of America, 1984), 1304-1310.

3

Leadership and the Love of God

"I have faith in order to understand."
—St. Augustine

As one examines the philosophical foundations of leadership in contemporary Western culture, it is somewhat unusual to find the teachings of St. Augustine included among the considerations of current scholars. Many philosophers would argue that his thought does not merit attention, for, after all, he was more a theologian than he was a philosopher. Certainly, they would be correct in their assertion. Augustine relied more heavily on faith than he did on reason as he drew his conclusions regarding the nature of the universe. Others, on the other hand, would argue that Augustine's works include numerous considerations of a strictly philosophic nature. As political historian Ernest Fortin explains, by extracting these considerations from their context, one can easily discern what could be properly regarded as his political philosophy:

> However, since Augustine himself . . . does not look upon philosophy as a self-contained and, in its own realm, independent discipline, or since he does not in fact deal with philosophy and theology as separate sciences, it seems preferable to respect the unity of his thought and to present his views on political matters as a single, coherent whole governed by theological principles.[1]

It seems quite appropriate, then, to consider his thoughts concerning the nature of leadership, especially in this election year as candidates are most outspoken regarding the importance of faith within the leadership dyad. More important, not to acknowledge his contributions would be to ignore a body of thought which would serve as a significant stabilizing force for more than a thousand years as Western culture suffered the anguish of intellectual stagnation through the Dark Ages. Without question, Augustine provides an important transition as we examine the philosophical foundations of leadership within our cultural heritage.

The thought of Augustine was heavily influenced by the teachings of his early Greek ancestors. Yet, the scenery that surrounded Plato and Aristotle bears little resemblance to the world in which we find St. Augustine some seven centuries later. Whereas the Greek philosophers had proposed leadership dyads consisting of small numbers of citizens ruled by philosopher-kings and virtuous men, Augustine was challenged to address the shattered remains of a crumbling Roman Empire. Small aristocratic city-states considered by Hellenistic philosophers to be natural in their origins had given way to an expansive, massive empire. Equally important, by the time of Augustine, the majesty that was Rome had ended. Caesar was no longer proclaimed to be God. The barbaric hordes from the North were in the final stages of destroying what remained of civilized society in Western Europe. This, then, is the political context in which we find Augustine at the beginning of the fifth century.

Two of the prominent philosophies of the period had their origins in Greece: Epicureanism and Stoicism. For Epicurus, the world had come into being quite by chance. There were no unifying principles. Known today as the Father of Hedonism, he taught that men not only *do* seek pleasure, but they *should* seek pleasure. The nature of man was not to pursue an *ideal good*. Rather, it was to avoid pain. Stoicism, however, was markedly different. It taught that divine reason acts on matter to provide order in the universe. Zeno had asserted that although man is *one* with this force, he can do nothing to alter it. The task of humans is to free themselves from their passions and emotions, their desires and wants, and align their wills with the will of the divine plan. If one is born to rule, that is one's fate. If one is born into slavery, so be it. If the empire falls, that is its destiny. Certainly, we can discern elements of Stoicism within the writings of St. Augustine.

Moreover, whereas the Greeks had provided him an understanding of the world based on the supremacy of reason, Augustine's intellectual framework regarding the meaning of law had its origins in Judaism and the Old Testament. At the same time, Christianity and the New Testament informed his teachings regarding the meaning of love within the context of human relationships. Each of these influences shaped his understanding regarding the nature of man.

Accordingly, each helped form what might have been his responses concerning the underlying questions of leadership. *Who should lead? What gives one the right to influence the behavior of others?*

Philosophically, Augustine was a Platonist. He was an *Idealist*, believing that an ideal form transcends our perceptions. It is unchanging. It is universal. It illuminates the shadows of darkness within the cave of human existence. For Plato, this form was the *Ideal*. For Augustine, it was *God*. Accordingly, in his work, *City of God*, Augustine explains that God created man to share in the *oneness* of the universe. In stark opposition to the teachings of Epicurus, Augustine taught that the nature of man was not to seek pleasure but to live in harmonious peace with his creator. He explains,

> This is prescribed by the order of nature: it is thus that God has created man. For 'let them,' He says, 'have dominion over the fish of the sea, and over the fowl of the air, and over every creeping thing which creepeth on the earth.' He did not intend that His rational creature, who was made in His image, should have dominion over anything but the irrational creation—not man over man, but man over the beasts.[2]

In Paradise, then, there was no leadership dyad among humankind. No person was to have authority over another. All were to share *equally* in His glory. Through original sin, however, Adam rejected God, and in doing so, corrupted the human race. He separated us from our creator. Thus, rather than enjoy a nature of *oneness* with their creator, the sons and daughters of Adam are doomed to suffer the pains of a fallen nature, and their only hope for reunification is through grace and salvation.

All is not lost, however, for according to Augustine, some of God's people have been chosen to share in His glory. They have been predestined to join Him once more in the heavenly kingdom. At the same time, others have been destined to suffer the loss of their original nature throughout eternity. Yet, both must reside on this earth until the day of judgment. Thus, when we are born, we are born to walk in one of two kingdoms. Some walk in the City of Man, a city based on self-love, deceit, and corruption. Others have been selected to walk in the City of God, a city based on the love and glory of the heavenly kingdom. And the lives we live reflect the city in to which we have been born. In *City of God* Augustine explains,

> This race we have distributed into two parts, the one consisting of those who live according to man, the other of those who live according to God. And these we also mystically call the two cities, or the two communities of men, of which the one is

predestined to reign eternally with God, and the other to suffer eternal punishment with the devil.[3]

Even though Augustine describes the City of Man as divided against itself, he does not hold that it is, in itself, inherently evil. It possesses the potential for goodness. To be sure, however, its promises are shallow, for its citizens rejoice in the goods of the earthly city rather than delight in the ultimate good of the heavenly kingdom. It is consumed with quarrel, with litigation, with war. Even its victories are life destroying or short-lived. Thus, it is incapable of bringing fulfillment to the soul of man.

Such is the nature of all earthly organizations. Such, too, is the nature of leadership within them. It is based on hostility. It is self-serving. It is destructive. Augustine, thus, does not explain so much who *should* lead. Instead, he more readily answers the question, who *does* lead in the City of Man? His answers are less than inspiring: the selfish, the unjust, the deceitful, the greedy; those who rejoice in the pursuit of trinkets and the pleasures of the flesh. This is the fallen nature of humanity within the City of Man, and those who must walk in this city are incapable of achieving the purposes of their nature.

Augustine believed that the purpose of all humans is to seek happiness, and the path to happiness is through the attainment of peace. Like Plato, he believed that the peace of all things lies in the tranquility of order, even if such order brings misery to our lives:

> Peace between man and God is the well-ordered obedience of faith to eternal law. Peace between man and man is well-ordered concord. Domestic peace is the well-ordered concord between those of the family who rule and those who obey. Civil peace is a similar concord among the citizens. The peace of the celestial city is the perfectly ordered and harmonious enjoyment of God, and of one another in God. . . . Order is the distribution which allots things equal and unequal, each to its own place. And hence, though the miserable, in so far as they are such, do certainly not enjoy peace, but are severed from that tranquility of order in which there is no disturbance, nevertheless, inasmuch as they are deservedly and justly miserable, they are by their very misery connected with order. [4]

Nevertheless, those who have been predestined to walk within the City of God while living on earth may still achieve happiness within their leadership positions. Some do. And when they do, they are readily recognizable. They seek justice; they seek goodness, not only for themselves, but for all who might be subject to their authority. Indeed, they lead in accordance with the love and mercy of God.

If, however, earthly peace is the well-ordered concord between those who rule and those who are ruled, what determines one's right to rule another? For Augustine, the answer is quite simple. Those who care for others should rule over those who are dependent upon their care. The emperor should rule his citizens. The master should rule his servants. Husbands should rule their wives. Parents should rule their children. And regardless of one's misery, all who are dependent should joyfully obey, for such obedience provides well-ordered concord within the society of fallen man. Similarly, those who rule should do so as servants. Augustine explains that "even those who rule serve those whom they seem to command, for they rule not from a love of power, but from a sense of the duty they owe to others—not because they are proud of authority, but because they love mercy."[5]

Nevertheless, within the City of Man, justice is rarely served. Good men and women are often forced to obey the commands of the wicked. This condition, however, did not trouble Augustine. No matter how miserable a slave, a wife, or a child might be, injustice is not reflective of the will of God. Instead, it reflects the injustice of a fallen nature. And whereas equality among men exists within the City of God, it does not, it cannot, exist within the City of Man. Besides, Augustine argues, being in bondage to another is not the worst of possibilities within the earthly city. One could be in bondage to lust, a bondage far more severe than being forced to obey the commands of the wicked:

> And beyond question it is a happier thing to be the slave of a man than of lust; for even this very lust of ruling, to mention no others, lays waste men's hearts with the most ruthless dominion. Moreover, when men are subjected to one another in a peaceful order, the lowly position does as much good to the servant as the proud position does harm to the master. But by nature, as God first created us, no one is the slave either of man or of sin. This servitude is, however, penal, and is appointed by that law which enjoins the preservation of the natural order and forbids its disturbance; for if nothing had been done in violation of that law, there would have been nothing to restrain by penal servitude. And therefore the apostle admonishes slaves to be subject to their masters, and to serve them heartily and with good-will, so that, if they cannot be freed by their masters, they may themselves make their slavery in some sort free, by serving not in crafty fear, but in faithful love, until all unrighteousness pass away, and all principality and every human power be brought to nothing, and God be all in all.[6]

As can be readily noted, Augustine's approach to leadership is, in many ways, similar to that of the early Greek philosophers. Even though Augustine is most pessimistic concerning those who rise to positions of leadership within the City of Man, the leader who walks in the City of God resembles Plato's philosopher-king. He is a man of virtue. He is committed to the good of his followers. In terms of justice, he seeks to live in accordance with the code of his soul.

The same is true of his followers. Just as Plato advocates that followers should always obey their philosopher-kings, Augustine proposes that those who are ruled should be joyfully obedient, even if their leaders are wicked and unjust, for such obedience assures the well-ordered concord of the state. It assures peace; it assures justice; it assures happiness.

Thus, Augustine's answers to our questions become more apparent. *Who should lead?* Those who have been predestined by God to lead. At the same time, he does not hold that virtuous men *will* lead, for in the earthly city, deceit and contempt, not goodness and virtue, prevail. Leadership in the City of Man is most often based on corruption and vice, on selfishness and greed. Indeed, Lord Acton would have found little argument with Augustine when he noted the relationship between absolute power and absolute corruption.

Certainly, there are many examples of those who portray Augustine's descriptions of leadership within the City of Man. When we hear leaders speak of a *dog eat dog* world, they are acknowledging life in the earthly city. Rarely do such leaders seek to serve, they seek to be served. They are slow to praise and quick to condemnation. They do not seek the good of their people; they seek only advantages to satisfy their selfish pleasures. Similarly, when leaders admonish others to *know their place*, they are affirming Augustine's understanding of the fallen nature of humanity. When they oppose the efforts of those attempting to alleviate servitude, when they justify slavery, when they participate in the persecution of those less fortunate than themselves, when they deny others the dignity of their humanness, they are acknowledging the observations of St. Augustine.

On a more positive note, when contemporary leaders seek justice for those placed in their care, they are reflecting leadership in accordance with those among our leaders who have been destined to walk in the City of God. Augustine describes them as follows:

> But we say that they are happy if they rule justly; if they are not lifted up amid the praises of those who pay them sublime honours, and the obsequiousness of those who salute them with an excessive humility, but remember that they are men; if they make their power the handmaid of His majesty by using it for the greatest possible extension of His worship; if they fear, love, worship God; if more than their own they love that

kingdom in which they are not afraid to have partners; if they are slow to punish, ready to pardon; if they apply that punishment as necessary to government and defence of the republic, and not in order to gratify their own enmity; if they grant pardon, not that iniquity may go unpunished, but with the hope that the transgressor may amend his ways; if they compensate with the lenity of mercy and the liberality of benevolence for whatever severity they may be compelled to decree; if their luxury is as much restrained as it might have been unrestrained; if they prefer to govern depraved desires rather than any nation whatever; and if they do all these things, not through ardent desire of empty glory, but through love of eternal felicity, not neglecting to offer to the true God, who is their God, for their sins, the sacrifices of humility, contrition, and prayer. Such of the reality itself, when that which we wait for shall have arrived.[7]

Are there such leaders among us? Of course. Yet, Augustine would suggest that they are few in number. And when we find them, they are often subjected to sneering and ridicule. They are attacked because *kindness* and *patience* and *forgiveness* and *mercy* and *benevolence* are often perceived to be indications of *weakness* by those within the City of Man whose hearts and souls have been decayed by the pursuit of power and pleasure.

These, then, are but a few of Augustine's contributions toward our understanding of leadership in Western culture. Certainly, they are significant, not because they introduce new theories through which we might approach our topic, but because they ask us to consider the dimensions of a fallen nature, the dimensions of good and evil, as we seek to understand the leadership dyad.

More important, perhaps, is the fact that his blending of faith and reason came at a time when humankind was about to discover exactly how far the fallen nature of man could fall. The Dark Ages were beginning to extinguish the lights of intellectual activity within the Western world, and it would be another eight centuries before they would be turned on again. And one of the few candles that would burn throughout this period would be the teachings of St. Augustine, Bishop of Hippo.

Notes

1.   Ernest L. Fortin, "St. Augustine," in Leo Strauss and Joseph Cropsey, eds., *History of Political Philosophy* 3rd. ed. (Chicago: University of Chicago Press, 1987), 178.
2.   St. Augustine, *City of God*, trans. Marcus Dods (New York: The Modern Library, 1950), 693.
3.   Ibid., 478-479.
4.   Ibid., 687-690.
5.   Ibid.
6.   Ibid., 694.
7.   Ibid., 178.

4

Leaders and Religious Prelates

"To be sure, the light of reason is placed by nature in every man, to guide him in his acts towards his end."
—*St. Thomas Aquinas*

As the United States moves through its presidential election processes, we are reminded once more of our deep concern regarding the separation of church and state in Western societies, for we as a nation are suspicious of candidates who appear to have aligned themselves with the teachings of religious authorities. Simply ask Bush, or Bauer, or Keyes. In a manner somewhat reminiscent of the presidential campaign of John F. Kennedy, each has borne intense scrutiny by those who fear even the slightest influence of religion within the realm of American politics.

Few find such fears surprising, however, for their origins are deeply rooted in our culture. They stem from an era when leaders found it quite appropriate to subject themselves to the leadership of God's representative on earth: the Vicar of Christ, the Pope. And while there are many historical events from which to explore these alliances, from a strictly philosophical perspective, their origins can be traced directly to the teachings of St. Thomas Aquinas.

As we examine the philosophical foundations of leadership in Western culture, however, it is important to consider briefly the intellectual climate of those 800 years between Augustine and Aquinas. Indeed, they were years of stifling suppression. Reason had been abandoned. There were few insights concerning the core questions of leadership: *What is the nature of man? Who should lead? What gives one the right to exact obedience from another?* With the Roman Catholic Church having become the ultimate source of authority in all matters, both religious and secular, faith and dogma had become the sole avenues through which men sought understanding of the universe. In brief, these years were the darkest of ages for Western Civilization.

By the thirteenth century, however, glimmerings of social progress were on the horizon. Feudalism was on the wane. The crusades had opened trade routes to the East, and cities were expanding throughout Western Europe. Gleams of intellectual light were beginning to sparkle from within those few universities that had emerged despite centuries of repression. Most significantly, having been preserved for centuries by Arabic cultures, Latin translations of the teachings of Aristotle began to seep in to Western thought once more. As a result, scholastics began to challenge the notion that the material world could be the cause of sin; they began to argue against the concept of a *fallen nature.* Although for the most part they maintained their allegiance to Christianity, their break from the teachings of Augustine nurtured seeds of change that would impact our understanding of leadership. And the most notable of these scholastic philosophers was St. Thomas Aquinas.

Like Aristotle, Aquinas was a *realist.* Although he believed in the *ideal*, he thought it to be *one* with the matter it informs. He shared Aristotle's proposition that what we perceive through our senses is not, as Plato had taught, a mere imitation of the *real* world. *It is the real world itself.* Thus, he drew a clear distinction between faith and reason, and in doing so, taught that the two are only different approaches to the same truth. They should not be viewed as contradictory, but as complementary to one another. Considering his philosophy to be the handmaiden of his theology, his thought is significant, for it signaled a major shift in the manner in which humans viewed themselves within the hierarchy of existence.

In terms of the nature of humans, Aquinas taught that our end is to be happy. Like Aristotle, he proposed that happiness cannot be found in carnal pleasure, or wealth, or glory. Yet, Aquinas ventured beyond Aristotle's teachings that it can be attained through the pursuit of truth and virtuous living, for he did not believe that knowledge obtained exclusively through the senses to be sufficient for one's understanding of the *Absolute*. Thus, he included faith as a part of his equation regarding the nature of humans. Although he agreed that reason might provide us a form of limited happiness, Aquinas taught that our ultimate happiness can only be achieved in the heavenly kingdom through the beatific vision. In his work *Summa Contra Gentiles* he relies on faith to support his conclusions:

> For man can arrive at a full understanding of the truth only by a sort of movement of inquiry; and he fails entirely to understand things that are by nature most intelligible, as we have proved. Therefore neither is happiness, in its perfect nature, possible to man; but he has a certain participation of it, even in this life. This seems to have been Aristotle's opinion about happiness. Hence, inquiring whether misfortunes destroy happiness, he shows that happiness seems especially to consist in deeds of virtue, which seem to be most stable in this life, and concludes that those who in this life attain to this perfection are happy *as men*, as though not attaining to happiness absolutely, but in a human way.
>
> * * *
>
> Therefore man's ultimate happiness will consist in that knowledge of God which the human mind possesses after this life, a knowledge similar to that by which separate substances know him. Hence our Lord promises us a *reward . . . in heaven* (*Matt.v.*12) and states (*Matt.xxii.*30) that the saints *shall be as the angels*, who always see God in heaven (*Matt.xviii.*10).[1]

Even though Aquinas taught that man's ultimate happiness consists in the contemplation of God, his political philosophy was rooted in natural law: "to the natural law belong those things to which a man is inclined naturally; and among these it is proper to man to be inclined to act according to reason."[2] He rejected Augustine's notion that deceit and greed and sin and evil lie at the heart of social relationships. In his work *On Kingship* he explains,

> To be sure, the light of reason is placed by nature in every man, to guide him in his acts towards his end. Wherefore, if man were intended to live alone, as many animals do, he would require no other guide to his end. Each man would be a king unto himself, under God, the highest King, inasmuch as he would direct himself in his acts by the light of reason given him from on high. Yet it is natural for man, more than any other animal, to be a social and political animal, to live in a group.
>
> This is clearly a necessity of man's nature. For all other animals, nature has prepared food, hair as a covering, teeth, horns, claws as means of defence or at least speed in flight, while man alone was made without any natural provisions for these things. Instead of all these, man was endowed with reason, by the use of which he could procure all these things for himself by the work of his hands. Now, one man alone is not able to procure them all for himself, for one man could not sufficiently provide for life, unassisted. It is therefore natural that man should live in the society of many.[3]

Not all within this society of interdependence, however, were of equal talents and abilities. Like Aristotle, he perceived a natural hierarchy among humans. Some were superior to others. There were freemen, those who are wise and virtuous. There were slaves, those who do not exist for their own sake, but for the sake of others. Accordingly, in the *Summa Contra Gentiles* he explains that the primary trait that gives leaders the right to exact obedience from their followers is the rational power of their respective intellects:

> And since man has both intellect and sense, and bodily power, these are ordered to one another, according to the disposition of the divine providence, in likeness to the order to be observed in the universe. For bodily power is subject to the powers of sense and intellect, as carrying out their commands; and the sensitive power is subject to the intellectual power, and is controlled by its rule.
>
> In the same way, we find order among men. For those who excel in intellect are naturally rulers, whereas those who are less intelligent, but strong in body, seem made by nature for service, as Aristotle says in his *Politics*. The statement of Solomon (*Prov*.xi.29) is in agreement with this: *The fool shall serve the wise*; as also the words of *Exodus* (xviii.21,22): *Provide out of all the people wise men such as fear God . . . who may judge the people at all times.*[4]

Aquinas also shared Aristotle's belief that although women participate in *humanness* with men, their functions in society are quite different. Whereas men are properly ordered toward intellectual activity, women are more ordered for reproduction. For Aquinas, these two common but distinct natures are brought to fulfillment through the act of coitus wherein the two are made one. Once again, in his *Summa Theologica* he supports his philosophy with theology:

> It was necessary for woman to be made, as the Scripture says, as *a helper* to man; not, indeed, as a helpmate in other works, as some say, since man can be more efficiently helped by another man in other works; but as a helper in the work of generation. . . . Among perfect animals, the active power of generation belongs to the male sex, and the passive power to the female. And as among animals there is a vital operation nobler than generation, to which their life is principally directed, so it happens that the male sex is not found in continual union with the female in perfect animals, but only at the time of coition; so that we may consider that by coition the male and female are one, as in plants they are always united, even though in some cases one of them preponderates, and in some the other. But man is further ordered to a still nobler work of life, and that is intellectual operation. Therefore there was greater reason for the distinction of these two powers in man; so that the female should be produced separately from the male, and yet that they should be carnally united for generation. Therefore directly after the formation of woman, it was said: *And they shall be two in one flesh* (*Gen*.ii.24).[5]

Given this distinction between the purposes for which men and women were created, Aquinas further proposes that the individual nature of women, that is, her *womanness*, is defective. A woman is a misbegotten man. Within their common nature, however, they are brought together as one in the act of generation. Nevertheless, although unified at coitus, women were created to be subservient to men:

As regards the individual nature, woman is defective and misbegotten, for the active power in the male seed tends to the production of a perfect likeness according to the masculine sex; while the production of woman comes from defect in the active power, or from some material indisposition, or even from some external influence, such as that of a south wind, which is moist, as the Philosopher observes. On the other hand, as regards universal human nature, woman is not misbegotten, but is included in nature's intention as directed to the work of generation. Now the universal intention of nature depends on God, Who is the universal Author of nature. Therefore, in producing nature, God formed not only the male but also the female.

Subjection is twofold. One is servile, by virtue of which a superior makes use of a subject for his own benefit; and this kind of subjection began after sin. There is another kind of subjection, which is called economic or civil, whereby the superior makes use of his subjects for their own benefit and good; and this kind of subjection existed even before sin. For the good of order would have been wanting in the human family if some were not governed by others wiser than themselves. So by such a kind of subjection woman is naturally subject to man, because in man the discernment of reason predominates.[6]

It is through this hierarchy of human inequality, then, that we can more readily delineate Aquinas' answers to the underlying question regarding leadership. *Who should lead?* Certainly, his answer would not include the less intelligent among us. It would not include those who are strong of body yet weak of mind. It would not include women. It would, instead, include only the freemen, those born with the intellectual capacity to understand and seek the common good of all within our society.

But who among the freemen should lead? In his commentary on Aristotle's *Politics,* Aquinas suggests that some are born with greater capacities for virtue than others, that leaders differ naturally from their followers through the possession of a certain greatness of goodness.[7] Thus, we might readily conclude that the one who possesses the highest level of goodness *should* lead. As we shall discover below, however, the person of high virtue is not always the one who *does* lead.

And Aquinas emphasizes the word *one.* He has little use for leadership by the *few,* much less by the *many.* Aristocracies are divisive, he explains. Democracies oppress the rich. In his work *On Kingship,* he explains that unity must be paramount, for it is the underlying reason for which societies are formed. Without unity, we have no peace. Without unity, we have no justice.

Now the welfare and safety of a multitude formed into a society lies in the preservation of its unity, which is called peace. If this is removed, the benefit of social life is lost and, moreover, the multitude in its disagreement becomes a burden to itself. The chief concern of the ruler of a multitude, therefore, is to procure the unity of peace.

***

> Among bees there is one king bee and in the whole universe there is One God, Maker and Ruler of all things. And there is reason for this. Every multitude is derived from unity. Wherefore, if artificial things are an imitation of natural things and a work of art is better according as it attains a closer likeness to what is in nature, it follows that it is best for a human multitude to be ruled by one person.[8]

At the same time, Aquinas acknowledges that not all leaders are just. Tyrants within our societies and organizations are often brutal and self-serving, seeking gain for themselves at the expense of their followers. Even so, Aquinas taught that tyranny is not the worst of conditions. It is preferable to disunity, for without unity, there is only chaos and anarchy. Consequently, revolution against tyranny held no stead in the teachings of St. Thomas Aquinas.

Instead, Aquinas taught that tyranny is a result of sin. It is punishment by God. Accordingly, the only recourse for tyranny lies in the hands of the Creator. Thus, to gain His mercy, those having been subjected to tyranny should not complain. They should not revolt. Instead, they should pay reverence to the tyrant, turn their backs on sin, and pray for forgiveness:

> But to deserve to secure this benefit from God, the people must desist from sin, for it is by divine permission that wicked men receive power to rule as a punishment for sin, as the Lord says by the Prophet Osee: 'I will give thee a king in my wrath' and it is said in *Job* that he 'maketh a man that is a hypocrite to reign for the sins of the people.' Sin must therefore be done away with in order that the scourge of tyrants may cease.[9]

Aquinas' understanding of the leadership dyad, then, blends the natural with supernatural; his philosophy complements his theology. And it is this complement of reason and faith that gives rise to his assertion that effective leaders should align themselves with the heavenly kingdom.

As noted above, he would agree that leaders should pursue truth and virtue. Yet, for Aquinas, these are but intermediate ends that can be attained through the senses. They can be achieved through reason. The ultimate end for humanity is the contemplation of God, however, and in order to achieve this end humans must reach beyond reason. Only faith allows us the beatific vision. Thus, in accordance with our ultimate end as humans, even the most notable of our leaders among earthly societies should align themselves with the representative of God's kingdom on earth, namely, the Vicar of Christ, the Roman Pontiff. In his book, *On Kingship*, he explains,

Yet through virtuous living man is further ordained to a higher end, which consists in the enjoyment of God, as we have said above. Consequently, since society must have the same end as the individual man, it is not the ultimate end of an assembled multitude to live virtuously, but through virtuous living to attain to the possession of God.

If this end could be attained by the power of human nature, then the duty of a king would have to include the direction of men to it. . . . But because a man does not attain his end, which is the possession of God, by human power but by divine–according to the words of the Apostle: 'By the grace of God life everlasting'–, therefore the task of leading him to that last end does not pertain to human but to divine government.

***

Thus, in order that spiritual things might be distinguished from earthly things, the ministry of this kingdom has been entrusted not to earthly kings but to priests, and most of all to the chief priest, the successor of St. Peter, the Vicar of Christ, the Roman Pontiff. To him all the kings of the Christian People are to be subject as to our Lord Jesus Christ Himself. For those to whom pertains the care of intermediate ends should be subject to him to whom pertains the care of the ultimate end, and be directed by his rule.[10]

In summary, then, we are able to discern more clearly Aquinas' understanding of the leadership dyad. First, all leadership should be aligned with the teachings of the kingdom of God. Second, only good and virtuous men should lead: the king over his realm; the master over his slave; the father over his children, and the husband over his wife. And followers should obey, for to disobey one's leader is to disobey God. Even tyranny is preferable to revolution and disunity. And should evil and less virtuous men rise to power, such events should be viewed as God's punishment for sin.

As we seek further illustrations of how Aquinas has contributed to our understanding of leadership, we need to look little further than to the influences of Aristotle. Although there are inherent differences in their philosophies, in many ways their thought is parallel. When we insist that our leaders be wise and virtuous, for example, when we demand that they seek the common good of all rather than pursue their particular selfish interests, we are expounding the teachings of these philosophical giants.

Similarly, both viewed the leadership dyad as a natural hierarchy. The more intelligent should lead. The less intelligent should follow. Physical prowess should be subservient to rational power. Women should subject themselves to the rule of men. Thus, when we justify inequalities based upon the accidents of one's birth, whether in our politics, our educational institutions, our corporate boardrooms, our sanctuaries, or our military organizations, we are standing squarely on the shoulders of Aristotle and Aquinas.

Likewise, Aquinas was in agreement with his Greek predecessors regarding the need for unity within our organizations. To be fragmented is to fail. It is the responsibility of leaders to assure unity within their organizations. Certainly, few leaders within Western civilization today would argue that tyranny is preferable to disunity. At the same time, many would be hesitant to allow organized dissent among their followers. Most would command obedience, regardless of the situation. And although they might encourage participation within the managerial process, they would join with Aquinas in his teachings of oneness and unity and the importance of hierarchy within their organizational structures.

Among the major distinctions regarding their thoughts on leadership, however, is the contention of Aquinas that noble and virtuous leaders should subject themselves to the rule of the Vicar of Christ in order that they might attain their ultimate end, that is, the contemplation of God and the beatific vision. Certainly, such a proposition would have been foreign to Aristotle. In terms of the leadership dyad, however, it is important, for within Western society, the concept has influenced both secular and religious leaders for centuries. Even in this era of democracies and egalitarianism, we find isolated incidences of leaders who willingly subject themselves to the teachings of religious prelates. More commonly, however, there are many who perceive a transcendence from the natural to the supernatural, a connection between themselves and the kingdom of heaven, and, thus, they lead in accordance with their religious beliefs. Indeed, such leadership is in keeping with the thoughts of Thomas Aquinas.

Certainly, the teachings of Aquinas are important as we seek a deeper understanding of leadership, for they demonstrate a continuity of political thought among Western societies. They highlight man's continued awareness of himself within a hierarchy of existence. They acknowledge his attempt to find unity within nature. They underscore his struggle to relate the universal to the specific, the transcendental to the real, the supernatural to the natural. More important, however, is that they reflect a deep respect for reason and natural law, reinforcing our belief that people are something more than mere subjects to blind faith. As a result, the teachings of Aquinas rekindled a spirit of individualism that would alter the course Western thought.

But it would be several centuries before such influences would reach their threshold. Other challenges would occur. There would be a return to the Christian love of Augustine by those who sought meaning and understanding through a less legalistic approach to the nature of the universe. Humanism would clash with rationalism. Reason would give way to faith; then again, faith to reason. Yet, because of St. Thomas Aquinas and the scholastic philosophers of the thirteenth century, the shackles of dogma had been loosened. The human intellect, its reason, had been set free, released from the suppressive bondage of the Dark Ages. Indeed, Western culture was preparing for a reformation, a renaissance, and an enlightenment unparalleled in its history.

Notes

1. Thomas Aquinas, "Summa Contra Gentiles," in *Basic Writings of Saint Thomas Aquinas*, ed. Anton C. Pegis, 2 vols. (New York: Random House, 1944) 2:86-87.
2. Thomas Aquinas," Summa Theologica" in *Basic Writings of Saint Thomas Aquinas* ed. Anton C. Pegis, ed., 2 vols. (New York: Random House, 1944), 2: 777.
3. Thomas Aquinas, *On Kingship*, trans. Gerald B. Phelan (Toronto: Pontifical Institute of Medieval Studies, 1949), 4.
4. Thomas Aquinas*, Summa Contra Gentiles*, 2:152-153.
5. Thomas Aquinas*, Summa Theologica*, I:879-880.
6. Ibid. 880-881.
7. Thomas Aquinas, "Commentary on the Politics," in *Medieval Political Philosophy*, eds. R. Lerner and M. Mahdi (New York: The Free Press, 1963), 330-331.
8. Thomas Aquinas, *Kingship*, 11-12.
9. Ibid. 29.
10. Ibid. 60-62.

5

The Divine Right of Kings

"Naturally, every man has right to every thing."
—Thomas Hobbes

Throughout the history of Western civilization, never, perhaps, has there been a period more rich and illuminating than the middle centuries of the second millennium. Accordingly, as we examine the philosophical foundations of leadership, the intellectual scenery gradually becomes more glorious as we travel from the years of St. Thomas Aquinas to those of Thomas Hobbes. By the time we reach the seventeenth century, Gutenberg will have printed his Bible. Columbus will have discovered America. Michelangelo will have completed his statue of David. Machiavelli will have shaken the political world with his discourse on power. Luther will have posted his ninety-five theses at Wittenburg. Henry VIII will have declared himself as supreme head of the English church. Shakespeare will have written *Hamlet*. Copernicus and Galileo and Kepler will have given humanity a new understanding of its position in the universe. A reformation, a renaissance, and a scientific revolution unparalleled in our history will have tempered the mind and the soul of humankind. In his book, *The Passion of the Western Mind*, Professor Richard Tarnas describes the period as follows:

> And so between the fifteenth and seventeenth centuries, the West saw the emergence of a newly self-conscious and autonomous human being–curious about the world, confident in his own judgments, skeptical of orthodoxies, rebellious against authority, responsible for his own beliefs and actions, enamored of the classical past but even more committed to a greater future, proud of his humanity, conscious of his distinctness from nature, aware of his artistic powers as individual creator, assured of his intellectual capacity to comprehend and control nature, and altogether less dependent on an omnipotent God.[1]

This is the world in which we find Thomas Hobbes, one in which the dynamics of intellectual curiosity and individual responsibility would forge a new understanding of how man would perceive himself and his relationship to others.

In terms of his philosophy, Thomas Hobbes was a rationalist. Deeply influenced by the inductive empiricism of Francis Bacon, he made no *a priori* assumptions about the nature of the universe. Since rationalism had been successful in revealing truths within the physical sciences, Hobbes held that the scientific method could be applied with equal success to human relationships. By understanding the laws of nature, he believed, man could understand his appropriate position within the leadership dyad.

Accordingly, he scoffed at the teachings of both Plato and Aristotle. For Hobbes, there was no *ideal*. There were no *transcendentals*. *Universals* were mere mental constructs that had nothing to do with the divine. Hobbes drew a clear distinction between philosophy and theology. If we want to understand nature, he taught, we must rely on reason. If we want to know about God, we must rely on faith and revelation. He separated the physical from the metaphysical. Consequently, his philosophy encompassed only the impersonal world of concrete experience.

Likewise, Machiavelli had significantly influenced his thought, for Hobbes gave little credence to political philosophies based upon assertions regarding man's ultimate purpose and final end. He did not begin with a premise as to what man *should* do. Instead, he based his conclusions upon his empirical observations as to what man *does* do. *Virtue* and *goodness* are not to be considered as *absolutes*, but only relative to one's experiences. What appears *good* to one may appear *evil* to another. Hobbes thus concluded that humans do not act in accordance with a final cause. Rather, they seek pleasure and avoid pain. They are driven by the passions of their nature, and these passions give rise to the formation of their social institutions.

It might be expected, then, that Hobbes would reject those teachings of St. Thomas Aquinas that viewed man as a political animal being drawn collectively toward virtue and the contemplation of God. Instead, he proposed that in a pure state of nature, there is no virtue; there is no goodness. Every man is the enemy of every other man. Humans live in a condition of constant fear, he taught, one being pitted against the other as they attempt to escape death. In the *Leviathan*, Hobbes describes the world of primitive man:

In such condition, there is no place for industry; because the fruit thereof is uncertain: and consequently no culture of the earth; no navigation, nor use of the commodities that may be imported by sea; no commodious building; no instruments of moving, and removing, such things as require much force; no knowledge of the face of the earth; no account of time; no arts; no letters; no society; and which is worst of all, continual fear, and danger of violent death; and the life of man, solitary, poor, nasty, brutish, and short.[2]

Interestingly, Hobbes does not attribute this state of continuous war and conflict to a condition of inequality among men. He does not hold that some are born superior to others, and, therefore, seek to subjugate those born with less talent and ability. On the contrary, he argues that *equality*, not *inequality*, lies at the core of man's struggle. It is because all men are *equal* that they believe they can attain their needs; it is because they are equal that no person, neither man nor woman, is willing to serve as the slave of another. Hobbes explains,

Nature hath made man so equal, in the faculties of the body, and mind; as that though there be found one man sometimes manifestly stronger in body, or of quicker mind than another; yet when all is reckoned together, the difference between man, and man, is not so considerable, as that one man can thereupon claim to himself any benefit, to which another may not pretend, as well as he. For as to the strength of body, the weakest has strength enough to kill the strongest, either by secret machination, or by confederacy with others, that are in the same danger with himself.

And as to the faculties of the mind, setting aside the arts grounded upon words, and especially that skill of proceeding upon general, and infallible rules, called science; which very few have, and but in few things; as being not a native faculty, born with us; nor attained, as prudence, while we look after somewhat else, I find yet a greater equality amongst men, than that of strength. For prudence, is but experience; which equal time, equally bestows on all men, in those things they equally apply themselves unto.[3]

Yet, out of this equality comes diffidence and mistrust, for no matter how strong or how intelligent one might be, when two people desire the same thing, they become enemies to one another. As a result, they live in fear that others will want what they have, whether it be their possessions or their lives. Thus, in the state of nature, humans can never be secure. There can be no trust. There can be no pleasure. There can be no justice. There can only be fear. In keeping with the proposals of Machiavelli, Hobbes describes the plight of humans as follows:

To this war of every man, against every man, this also is consequent; that nothing can be unjust. The notions of right and wrong, justice and injustice have there no place. Where there is no common power, there is no law: where no law, no injustice. Force, and fraud, are in war the two cardinal virtues. Justice, and injustice are none of the faculties neither of the body, nor mind. If they were, they might be in a man that were alone in the world, as well as his senses, and passions. They are qualities, that relate to men in society, not in solitude. It is consequent also to the same condition, that there be no propriety, no dominion, no *mine* and *thine* distinct; but only that to be every man's, that he can get: and for so long, as he can keep it.[4]

Thus, in order to escape his natural state of war, primitive man, Hobbes taught, was driven by his natural passions to seek peace. Fear and hope had motivated him to join his fellow men in order that they, together, might protect themselves from each other:

The passions that incline men to peace, are fear of death; desire of such things as are necessary to commodious living; and a hope by their industry to obtain them. And reason suggesteth convenient articles of peace, upon which men may be drawn to agreement. These articles, are they, which otherwise are called the Laws of Nature.[5]

Hobbes' laws of nature, however, differed from those of his classical Greek ancestors. His natural law did not direct and inspire civil law. There was no divine revelation against which to measure justice. In fact, many argue that his natural laws were not *laws* at all. They were *rights*. They did not forbid. Conversely, they provided liberty. They were man's source of freedom.

Drawing a distinction between a *right* and a *law*, Hobbes held that all people have the right to do *anything* necessary for their self-preservation. This *right* is his first *law* of nature. No person or social institution has the authority to deny any man this liberty. Accordingly, he concluded that *every* person has the right to *every* thing in order to maintain this liberty. In the *Leviathan* he explains,

And because the condition of man . . . is a condition of war of every one against every one; in which case every one is governed by his own reason; and there is nothing he can make use of, that may not be a help unto him, in preserving his life against his enemies; it followeth, that in such a condition, every man has a right to every thing; even to one another's body. And therefore, as long as this natural right of every man to every thing endureth, there can be no security to any man, how strong or wise soever he be, of living out the time, which nature ordinarily alloweth men to live. And consequently it is a precept, or general rule of reason, *that every man, ought to endeavour peace, as far as he has hope of obtaining it; and when he cannot obtain it, that he may seek, and use, all helps, and advantages of war*. The first branch of which rule, containeth the first, and fundamental law of nature; which is, *to seek peace, and follow it*. The second, the sum of the right of nature; which is, *by all means we can, to defend ourselves*.[6]

From this premise, Hobbes derived his second law of nature: *"that a man be willing, when others are so too, as far-forth, as for peace, and defence of himself he shall think it necessary, to lay down this right to all things; and be contented with so much liberty against other men, as he would allow other men against himself."* [7]

In brief, Hobbes concluded that within our primitive state, we live in constant fear, and the first law of nature provides us the right and liberty to do anything we deem necessary in order to defend and protect ourselves. At the same time, in order to achieve peace, nature gives us the liberty to set aside this right and form a covenant agreeing not to do harm to one other. Paraphrasing the Golden Rule, Hobbes suggested that it is natural for humans to agree *not* to do unto others what they would *not* have others do unto them.

According to Hobbes, one can set aside his right to do anything he wishes in one of two ways: either by renouncement or by transfer. If one agrees to renounce his right, he simply gives it up. All within the covenant do the same. On the other hand, we can willingly choose to transfer our rights to another whom we believe is capable of defending us. We can forfeit our rights to gain protection. Once they have been transferred to another, however, the covenant cannot be broken. Having transferred our rights, it is our duty to obey.

Nevertheless, Hobbes taught that some rights are beyond negotiation. No man, for example, can be forced to do anything he perceives to be harmful to himself. No man can give away his right to resist arrest or confinement. No man can be asked to wound another. He explains,

> And therefore there be some rights, which no man can be understood by any words, or other signs, to have abandoned, or transferred. As first a man cannot lay down the right of resisting them, that assault him by force, to take away his life; because he cannot be understood to aim thereby, at any good to himself. The same may be said of wounds, and chains, and imprisonment; both because there is no benefit consequent to such patience; as there is to the patience of suffering another to be wounded, or imprisoned: as also because a man cannot tell, when he seeth men proceed against him by violence, whether they intend his death or not. [8]

This covenant wherein humans willingly transfer their rights of liberty to others, then, is the foundation of Hobbes' society. It is the foundation of his civil law. For our purposes, it is the foundation of leadership, for those to whom these rights have been transferred have full authority to command obedience from those who seek their protection.

It should be noted, however, that even though one's rights might have been transferred to the sovereign, the leader is not part of the social contract itself, for the contract is only among those who have willingly agreed to the covenant, those who are to be protected. Moreover, since the sovereign makes the law, he is above the law; his authority is not to be questioned; his decisions cannot be challenged. He maintains his authority until such time that he can no longer protect the commonwealth in the *war of all against all*. Hobbes explains,

> The only way to erect such a common power, as may be able to defend them from the invasion of foreigners, and the injuries of one another, and thereby to secure them in such sort, as that by their own industry, and by the fruits of the earth, they may nourish themselves and live contentedly; is, to confer all their power and strength upon one man, or upon one assembly of men, that may reduce all their wills, by plurality of voices, unto one will: which is as much as to say, to appoint one man, or assembly of men, to bear their person; and every one to own, and acknowledge himself to be author of whatsoever he that so beareth their person, shall act, or cause to be acted, in those things which concern the common peace and safety; and therein submit their wills, every one to his will, and their judgments, to his judgment . . . as if every man should say to every man, *I authorize and give up my right of governing myself, to this man, or to this assembly of men, on this condition, that thou give up thy right to him, and authorize all his actions in like manner.*[9]

Having established this natural evolution of social institutions, the answers to our questions regarding leadership become more apparent: *Who should lead? What gives one the right to exact obedience from another? What are the rights of those being led?* In simple terms, for Hobbes, one's ability to provide *protection* determines who should lead. *Fear* gives one the right to exact obedience from another. Leadership is rooted exclusively in one's ability to protect followers from themselves as well as their adversaries, and with the exception of those individual liberties that cannot be transferred, the rights of followers are forfeited to the sovereign. They must pay homage even if the leader is a tyrant, for according to Hobbes, tyranny is preferable to man's condition in his primitive state of nature. He explains,

> And though of so unlimited a power, men may fancy many evil consequences, yet the consequences of the want of it, which is perpetual war of every man against his neighbour, are much worse. The condition of man in this life shall never be without inconveniences; but there happeneth in no commonwealth any great inconvenience, but what proceeds from the subject's disobedience, and breach of those covenants, from which the commonwealth hath its being. And whosoever thinking sovereign power too great, will seek to make it less, must subject himself, to the power, that can limit it; that is to say, to a greater.[10]

Of course, Hobbes did not consider obedience within this covenant to be an infringement upon individual rights, upon individual freedoms, for he believed that we willingly do what we perceive we must do in order to protect ourselves from our natural enemies. Although we may prefer not to transfer our rights, because we are afraid, we choose to do so: "when a man throweth his goods into the sea for *fear* the ship should sink," he explains, "he doth it nevertheless very willingly, and may refuse to do it if he will: it is therefore the action of one that was *free*."[11] Likewise, in a commonwealth men freely exchange their natural liberties for the peace and protection of the leader.

However dismal and bleak such an arrangement might appear, it should be noted that according to Hobbes, man's greatest freedom is not embedded in law, but in the *silence of law*. "In cases where the sovereign has prescribed no rule," he explains, "there the subject hath the liberty to do, or forbear, according to his own discretion."[12] In brief, followers are free to do anything they wish as long as there is no law against it. Thus, his social contract imposes few infringements on our daily lives, for in most of our activities, there are no laws against our behavior. As the law is silent, so, too are we free.

In response to our questions regarding those who should lead within our societies, Hobbes made no distinction between men and women. Although he believed men to be more fitted "for actions of labour and danger," he also held that humans are equal. "And whereas some have attributed the dominion to the man only, as being of the more excellent sex; they misreckon in it," he writes. "For there is not always that difference of strength, or prudence between the man and the woman, as that the right can be determined without war."[13] Women are as capable as men in their ability to instill fear.

Perhaps, the most seemingly incongruent facet of Hobbes' understanding of the leadership dyad, however, is his assertion that freedom of religion must not be tolerated within a society. Although many have questioned his motives, in the later chapters of the *Leviathan*, Hobbes notes that the king is God's only representative on earth. Such a proposal would hardly seem appropriate to a rationalist, to one who had been accused of atheistic totalitarianism. Indeed, his critics suggest that such a doctrine was most convenient for Hobbes at a time of religious turbulence when the populace was in a state of uprising against its king. Regardless, his teachings gave rise to the concept of the divine right of kings within Western society. In defense of his king against the attacks of the papacy, Hobbes held that the authority of the king is the authority of God; it cannot be questioned; there can be no appeal to a higher power. To disobey the king is to disobey God:

> If a man therefore should ask a pastor, in the execution of his office, as the chief-priests and elders of the people (*Matt.*xxi.23) asked our Savior, *By what authority doest thou these things, and who gave thee this authority?* he can make no other just answer, but that he doth it by the authority of the commonwealth, given him by the king, or assembly that representeth it. All pastors, except the supreme, execute their charges in the right, that is by the authority of the civil sovereign, that is *jure civili.* But the king, and every other sovereign, executeth his office of supreme pastor by immediate authority from God, that is to say, in *God's right* or *jure divino.* And therefore none but kings can put into their titles a mark of their submission to God only, *Dei gratia rex, &c.*[14]

Undoubtedly, the influence of Thomas Hobbes regarding our understanding of leadership is significant, for he was among the first in Western civilization to construct a covenant among followers within the dyad, a covenant based on the dark side of humanity. He expanded the practical advice of Machiavelli to his prince into a systematic discourse on human relationships. When we read Hobbes we find little mention of goodness, or beauty, or altruism. Instead, we find hostility, and chaos, and conflict. According to Hobbes, leadership is not based on a vision of the common good. It is based on *fear.* It is based on *fraud.* One's ability to lead is measured in terms of his ability to protect his followers from themselves. In many ways, leadership under Hobbes is similar to leadership within Augustine's City of Man. It is rooted in deception and despair.

Certainly, within the more developed societies of our culture, there are decreasing numbers of examples regarding the leadership dyad of Hobbes. Few nations in the Western world continue to base the authority of their leaders on the divine right of kings. Nevertheless, many leaders assume highly authoritative postures within their companies and organizations in a manner that resembles the monarchs of Thomas Hobbes. They are self-serving. They are self-indulgent. Their concern is not the well being of their employees; it is simply to maintain power, whether through fear or fraud or deceit. They command blind obedience from their people. They are not to be questioned, for it is their belief that challenged authority can only lead to chaos, and within a state of chaos, neither jobs nor people can be adequately protected. As in the *Leviathan*, employees have few liberties within these authoritarian organizations, for in the minds of the executives, individuals have set aside their rights as a condition of employment. Exceptions to the employee rights granted by management are not to be tolerated.

Except in the more underdeveloped societies of Western culture, authoritarianism within our organizations, however, seems to be on the wane. With leadership styles based on participation and delegation proving to be more productive in terms of effectiveness and efficiency, fear is used less frequently as a motivational tool. Followers are not threatened. They are respected. They are not coerced. They are nurtured and encouraged to develop their individual talents.

Nevertheless, there continue to be sweatshop environments where leaders capitalize on the innate fears of those who live on the margins of our society. There continue to be leaders who link their civil authority to heavenly authority. There continue to be those who advocate a dog-eat-dog perspective regarding human relationships. Whether such leaders function in political organizations, corporations, religious groups, or other social institutions, the philosophical foundation of their leadership can be traced directly to the writings of Thomas Hobbes.

The teachings of Hobbes, however, would not go unquestioned. His understanding of natural law and individual rights would be challenged. The meaning of a social contract would be debated. For the revolution in political thought brought about by the reformation and the renaissance did not end with Thomas Hobbes. The enlightenment of Western man was just beginning, and those who would follow Hobbes would reshape our understanding of the leadership dyad. Not only would the impact of their thought threaten authority throughout Europe, it would fuel the fire of an American revolution.

Notes

1.   Richard Tarnas, *The Passion of the Western Mind* (New York: Ballantine Books, 1991), 282.
2.   Thomas Hobbes, *Leviathan* (New York: Collier Books, Macmillan Publishing Company, 1962), 100.
3.   Ibid., 98.
4.   Ibid., 101.
5.   Ibid., 102.
6.   Ibid., 103-104.

7.   Ibid., 104.
8.   Ibid., 105.
9.   Ibid., 132.
10.   Ibid., 157.
11.   Ibid., 159-160.
12.   Ibid., 166.
13.   Ibid., 152.
14.   Ibid., 394-395.

6

Locke on Leadership:
The Abolishment of Privilege

*"Men living together according to reason, without a common superior on earth with
authority to judge between them, is properly the state of nature."*
—John Locke

In our search for understanding of the philosophical underpinnings of leadership, the seventeenth century provides a most fertile
environment for the exploration of new ideas. And by the time it
drew to a close, an intellectual awakening of the Western mind had
reached explosive proportions within the political arena of Europe.
Within less than fifty years in England, for example, the parliament
had defied the king; Cromwell had died; Charles II had returned to
the throne; William of Orange had led the Glorious Revolution against
James II; the crown had passed to William and Mary. A bill of rights
had struggled through the British Parliament, and the divine right of
British kings had been abolished. England had become the first major
constitutional monarchy in the Western world. Power and authority
had been pulled downward through the leadership dyad.

Deeply nestled in the spirit of this revolution were the writings of
John Locke: *Two Treatises of Civil Government.* The first was written in response to Sir Robert Filmer's *Patriarcha,* a defense of the
king, claiming that no person is born free, that all government is an
absolute monarchy. The second was written to delineate a political
philosophy that would serve as the inspiration for revolutions, not
only in Europe, but also in America. Both served as major forces in
altering our understanding of leadership.

Philosophically, Locke was a realist. Like Aristotle, he posited
that man's knowledge comes only through his senses. There are no

innate *ideas* as Plato had suggested. As a duelist, however, he rejected Aristotle's proposition regarding the *oneness* of matter and form. Although he argued there are two types of substances, mind and body, he believed them to be distinct from one another. Thus, he taught that as we experience sensations, our thoughts and our body, our mind and our passions, interact with one another, and through this interaction, we begin to know and understand the laws of nature and the divine forces that set it in motion. In brief, to know the laws of nature is to know the laws of God. Consequently, his approach to the leadership dyad begins with his understanding of the nature of humankind.

Although his conclusions were markedly different from those of Thomas Hobbes, there were similarities among their observations. Both, for example, viewed civil society as an avenue for securing peace among men; both believed in a natural desire for self-preservation; both held that humans were free and equal within the primitive state of nature; both believed that an ordered society is in the best interest of all. However, while Hobbes based his ordered society on passions of fear, Locke viewed the nature of humans quite differently. He taught that in their natural state, humans are relatively peaceful. Reason, he believed, not fear, teaches us to seek life, liberty, and the protection of our possessions, not only for ourselves, but for all mankind. In his work *The Second Treatise on Civil Government* he explains,

> The state of Nature has a law of Nature to govern it, which obliges every one, and reason, which is that law, teaches all mankind, who will but consult it, that being all equal and independent, no one ought to harm another in his life, health, liberty or possessions: for men being all the workmanship of one omnipotent, and infinitely wise Maker; all the servants of one sovereign Master, sent into the world by His order, and about His business; they are His property, whose workmanship they are, made to last during His, not one another's pleasure: . . . Every one, as he is bound to preserve himself, and not to quit his station willfully, so by the like reason, when his own preservation comes not in competition, ought he as much as he can to preserve the rest of mankind, and not unless it be to do justice on an offender, take away, or impair the life, or what tends to the preservation of the life, the liberty, health, limb or goods of another.[1]

Thus, in our natural state, we are not, as Hobbes had suggested, enemies to our neighbors. We are friends. No person exists for the pleasure of another. As creatures of God, humans not only seek to preserve themselves, reason teaches them to protect the lives of others as well. Although Locke suggested that our passions often promote self-interest, he was quite optimistic regarding our ability to cooperate and collaborate rather than confront and compete. As reason enlightens our passions, he argued, it leads us to conclude that it is in our best self-interest to do so.

Locke had earlier established the principle of self-preservation in his *First Treatise on Civil Government* as he explained that reason is the voice of God revealing to us the laws of nature:

> God having made man, and planted in him, as in all other animals, a strong desire of self-preservation, and furnished the world with things fit for food and raiment and other necessaries of life, subservient to His design that man should live and abide for some time upon the face of the earth, . . . for the desire, strong desire, of preserving his life and being having been planted in him as a principle of action by God Himself, reason, 'which was the voice of God in him,' could not but teach him and assure him that, pursuing that natural inclination he had to preserve his being, he followed the will of his Maker.[2]

Similarly, Locke argued that within this natural state, no person has power over another. Man's freedom to order his actions is directly linked to the laws of nature as ordained by the will of God. He explains in *The Second Treatise on Civil Government,*

> To understand political power aright, and derive it from its original, we must consider, what state all men are naturally in, and that is, a state of perfect freedom to order their actions, and dispose of their possessions and persons, as they think fit, within the bounds of the law of Nature, without asking leave, or depending upon the will of any other man.
>
> A state also of equality, wherein all the power and jurisdiction is reciprocal, no one have more than another; there being nothing more evident, than that creatures of the same species and rank, promiscuously born to all the same advantages of Nature, and the use of the same faculties, should also be equal one amongst another without subordination or subjection, unless the lord and master of them all should, by any manifest declaration of his will, set one above another, and confer on him, by an evident and clear appointment, an undoubted right to dominion and sovereignty.[3]

Similarly, Locke's thought regarding one's right to personal property is rooted in natural law. Accordingly, it is based upon the will of God. Unlike Hobbes who had proposed that there is *no thine and mine* unless it be acquired by fear and force and fraud, Locke insisted that labor establishes one's right to property. Since it is the result of one's personal labor, it is, therefore, a part of the person himself:

> Though the earth and all inferior creatures be common to all men, yet every man has a 'property' in his own 'person.' This nobody has any right to but himself. The 'labour' of his body and the 'work' of his hands, we may say, are properly his. Whatsoever,

then, he removes out of the state that Nature hath provided and left it in, he hath mixed his labour with it, and joined to it something that is his own, and thereby makes it his property. It being by him removed from the common state Nature placed it in, it hath by this labour something annexed to it that excludes the common right of other men. For this 'labour' being the unquestionable property of the labourer, no man but he can have a right to what that is once joined to, at least where there is enough, and as good left in common for others.[4]

Nevertheless, having delineated these laws of nature regarding man's right to life, liberty, and personal property, Locke recognized that humans often violate the dictates of reason. Men, for example, kill one another; they steal; the strong often go unpunished. And whereas Hobbes had proposed that such behavior was a result of fear, Locke held it to be the result of three basic deficiencies within nature itself.

First, he noted, there are no established laws within the primitive state, laws agreed upon by common consent, laws that could serve as a standard as to what is right and wrong. Even though natural law is plain and intelligible to all rational creatures, he suggests, there are those who are either biased in their interests or who are unwilling to study its directives. Second, Locke noted that nature lacks indifferent and unbiased judges, and the result is disorder and confusion: "self-love will make men partial to themselves and their friends; and on the other side, ill nature, passion, and revenge will carry them too far in punishing others, and hence nothing but confusion and disorder will follow."[5] Finally, he suggested, in the primitive state of nature, there is a lack of power for the administration of justice. Those with force often abuse the rights of others; yet, one whose life, liberty, or possessions have been violated has the natural right to punish his transgressor. Thus, Locke argued that it is reasonable for men to enter into a social contract to eliminate these deficiencies, and it is this covenant that serves as the foundation of civil society. It is this covenant that lies at the core of his leadership dyad.

The social contract of Locke, however, bears little resemblance to that proposed by Thomas Hobbes. Hobbes had suggested that humans enter into a contract among themselves, transferring their rights to the king in order to gain protection, not only from each other, but from other sovereignties as well. Yet, the king is not a party to the contract. He is the sovereign. Since he makes the laws, he is above the laws, and he maintains complete authority until such time that he can no longer protect the commonwealth.

Locke, however, considered such an arrangement to be inconsistent with the purposes of civil society, for it did not address the deficiencies of nature. Its laws were arbitrary. It did not provide for unbiased judges to settle disputes, for if the king were considered to be above the law, he could not administer the law in a just manner. Consequently, Locke believed it to be inevitable that the monarch would be in a constant state of war with his subjects, and even though a contract might have been drawn, people would remain in their primitive state. Hence, for Locke, a monarchy could be no form of government at all.

Consequently, at the heart of Locke's social contract lie remedies to these deficiencies. Accordingly, he addressed the first principle necessary for justice among men: clearly stated laws providing a standard for proper behavior enacted only through the consent of the governed. These laws cannot be arbitrary. They must apply to all. The lives, liberties, and possessions of all men must be protected:

> The great end of men's entering into society being the enjoyment of their properties in peace and safety, and the great instrument and means of that being the laws established in that society, the first and fundamental positive law of all commonwealths is the establishing of the legislative power, as the first and fundamental natural law which is to govern even the legislative. Itself is the preservation of the society and (as far as will consist with the public good) of every person in it. This legislative is not only the supreme power of the commonwealth, but sacred and unalterable in the hands where the community have once placed it.[6]

Locke's civil society also addressed the second deficiency of nature: impartiality regarding the settlement of differences among citizens. In his social contract, penalties were not arbitrarily determined; they were established by law. The community was the common judge of disputes, and those united through this agreement escaped this deficiency of nature:

> But because no political society can be, nor subsist, without having in itself the power to preserve the property, and in order thereunto punish the offences of all those of that society, there, and there only, is political society where every one of the members hath quitted this natural power, resigned it up into the hands of the community in all cases that exclude him not from appealing for protection to the law established by it. And thus all private judgment of every particular member being excluded, the community comes to be umpire, and by understanding indifferent rules and men authorised by the community for their execution, decides all the differences that may happen between any members of that society concerning any matter of right, and punishes those offences which any member hath committed against the society with such penalties as the law has established; whereby it is easy to discern who are, and are not, in political society together. Those who are united into one body, and have a common established law and

judicature to appeal to, with authority to decide controversies between them and punish offenders, are in civil society one with another; but those who have no such common appeal, I mean on earth, are still in the state of Nature, each being where there is no other, judge for himself and executioner; which is, as I have before showed it, the perfect state of Nature.[7]

Consequently, with leadership based upon the consent of the governed, Locke believed that society would have sufficient power and authority to enact its laws. No individual would have the force necessary to overrule the will of the people. Justice could be administered fairly. By each making himself subject to laws agreed upon by the people, order would be maintained. Thus, man would escape the deficiencies of his natural state and be free to enjoy the liberties given him by his creator.

Having reviewed Locke's framework for a civil society, we can address his understanding of leadership. Who among those who have willingly agreed to a covenant based upon consensual law should lead? Locke's answer to the question is far more complex than it might appear, for within his society all authority ultimately resides in the people.

Even when we select those who will represent us in matters of law, we do not transfer our right to lead ourselves. We merely entrust our representatives to carry out our wishes. Representatives become servants of the people. Should this trust be broken, the people maintain the right and authority to remove them. And although a legislature might appear to have supreme power, those who hold such power are always subject to the will of the people. Locke explains,

For all power given with trust for the attaining an end being limited by that end, whenever that end is manifestly neglected or opposed, the trust must necessarily be forfeited, and the power devolve into the hands of those that gave it, who may place it anew where they shall think best for their safety and security. And thus the community perpetually retains a supreme power of saving themselves from the attempts and designs of anybody, even of their legislators, whenever they shall be so foolish or so wicked as to lay and carry on designs against the liberties and properties of the subject.[8]

Similarly, Locke recognized the need for a separation of the power among those who are entrusted to serve through the consent of the followers. Those who make the laws, he believed, should not execute the laws. The temptation for injustice would be too great for those empowered by their positions.

From a purely theoretical perspective, then, there are no leaders within Locke's civil society. There are only trustees. There are only servants. Their function is not to lead but to enact the will of the people. Consequently, the rights of leaders are no different from the rights of followers. No more. No less. Leaders have no privilege. All have the right to life, liberty, and personal property. No person is subject to the will of another, and the laws of society guarantee that these rights will be protected.

Nevertheless, Locke acknowledged the obvious inequalities among humans. Age and virtue and rational ability often give some a natural advantage over others. Parents, for example, have the natural right of rule over their children until such time that age and reason deliver them from their subjugation. Locke explains,

> Thus we are born free as we are born rational; not that we have actually the exercise of either: age that brings one, brings with it the other too. And thus we see how natural freedom and subjection to parents may consist together, and are both founded on the same principle. A child is free by his father's title, by his father's understanding, which is to govern him till he hath it of his own.

* * *

> The freedom then of man, and liberty of acting according to his own will, is grounded on his having reason, which is able to instruct him in that law he is to govern himself by, and make him know how far he is left to the freedom of his own will. To turn him loose to an unrestrained liberty, before he has reason to guide him, is not the allowing him the privilege of his nature to be free, but to thrust him out amongst brutes, and abandon him to a state as wretched and as much beneath that of a man as theirs.[9]

As for differences among men and women, Locke was quite egalitarian in his teachings. Although he acknowledged that because of their different aptitudes and abilities a sort of inequality appears to exist between husbands and wives, he held that these differences in themselves do not warrant subjection by either. For Locke, any inequality that might exist between them would be those willingly agreed to within the marital contract. Since either may choose to enter into or break the contract, the husband has no more power over his wife than she has over him:

> But the husband and wife, though they have but one common concern, yet having different understandings, will unavoidably sometimes have different wills too. It therefore being necessary that the last determination (*i.e.,* the rule) should be placed somewhere, it naturally falls to the man's share as the abler and the stronger. But this, reaching but to the things of their common interest and property, leaves the wife in the full and true possession of what by contract is her peculiar right, and at least gives the husband no more power over her than she has over his life; the power of the husband being so far from that of an absolute monarch that the wife has, in many cases, a liberty

to separate from him where natural right or their contract allows it, whether that contract be made by themselves in the state of Nature or by the customs or laws of the country they live in, and the children, upon such separation, fall to the father or mother's lot as such contract does determine.[10]

Men, then, are not superior to women. Husbands and wives merely alter their freedoms in terms of a marriage contract to which they both voluntarily agree.

In a similar manner, Locke taught that one might willingly exchange his freedom for benefits another might provide. We might, for example, agree to exchange our labor for money. During the time we are in such employment, we agree to subject our will to that of another; we *consent* to be a servant within the leadership dyad. Even though we might exchange services for salary, however, our God given rights regarding life, liberty, and possessions remain intact:

For a free man makes himself a servant to another by selling him for a certain time the service he undertakes to do in exchange for wages he is to receive; and though this commonly puts him into the family of his master, and under the ordinary discipline thereof, yet it gives the master but a temporary power over him, and no greater than what is contained in the contract between them.[11]

Locke also understood the inequalities related to the possession of private property. In brief, Locke held that God gave the world to humans in common in order that they might improve on it. He also believed that those who develop these common gifts of God are justly entitled to the fruits of their labors. Yet, he was an optimist regarding the distribution of wealth, arguing that man would take no more of God's common gifts than he might need. Why would one hoard while others are without? Reason would dictate the foolishness of gathering more perishables than one could eat, for the food would only rot, depriving others of its nourishment. Yet, no matter how much man took from nature, humankind would always expand its yield through labor and invention. As a result, Locke believed that through man's effort, wasted and barren lands would be continuously developed into prosperous fields. Through man's creativity, the fruits of nature would always blossom.

Such are a few of the contributions of John Locke regarding our understanding of leadership in Western culture. First, Locke forced us to reconsider our understanding of the nature of humankind. In accordance with the dignity of reason, he taught that we have within us the ability to lead ourselves. People need not be dependent upon others to bring peace and unity to their lives. Equally significant, he taught that all humans, regardless of wealth or status, have liberties afforded them by their creator, and that no person has the power to infringe upon those rights. Indeed, with John Locke, the leadership dyad had been laid on its side.

In his essay on Locke, Robert Goldwin summarizes Locke's contributions to Western thought as follows:

> Locke sought to free mankind from every form of absolute arbitrary power. He sought to present the true and complete account of man's making of civilization out of the almost worthless materials furnished to him. In this account, the chief force that spurs man on to his own liberation is a passion, the desire for preservation. As the reader of this volume well knows, the ancient political philosophers considered the passions arbitrary and tyrannical; they thought that the tendency of the passions is, above all, to enslave men. They taught, therefore, that a man is free only to the extent that the reason in him is able, one way or another, to subdue and rule his passions. But Locke recognized passion as the supreme power in human nature and argued that reason can do no more than serve the most powerful and universal desire and guide it to its fulfillment. Only when this ordering of things is understood and accepted as the true and natural ordering is there any prospect of success in mankind's struggle for freedom, peace, and plenty. That, above all else, is Locke's political teaching.[12]

For Americans the implications of these teachings regarding their understanding of leadership are all too obvious, for Locke's writings served as the philosophical foundation of our independence as a nation. When Thomas Jefferson wrote, *We hold these truths to be self-evident, that all men are created equal, that they are endowed by their Creator with certain inalienable rights, that among these are Life, Liberty, and the pursuit of Happiness,* he was citing the teachings of John Locke. When the founding fathers of the United States drafted a constitution calling for separate and limited powers, they were acknowledging their understanding of John Locke. When capitalists defend their right to private property based on their initiatives, they are voicing their agreement with the writings of John Locke. So, too, are workers when they insist that the added value of their labors be acknowledged within a context of economic justice. Perhaps no other philosopher has had a greater influence regarding our understanding of political relationship in the United States than has John Locke, for his spirit permeates every crevice of this democracy.

And his influence is not limited to politics. It has impacted our understanding of leadership in the corporate world as well. Throughout the last fifty years there has been a growing movement toward participation and empowerment throughout all levels of our organizations. This is not to suggest that our companies and businesses have become democracies. They have not. It is, however, to note that increasing numbers of leaders are abandoning authoritative management styles in favor of those that respect the intelligence of their employees. They cooperate and collaborate with their people rather than confront and compete. They recognize a relationship between management and its employees that is structured by a social contract based upon inalienable rights afforded to all men by their creator. Such practices may be traced directly to a philosophy of man that acknowledges the dignity of humankind. They can be traced directly to the teachings John Locke.

The same is true in terms of *equality*. Even though many Western democracies were founded upon Locke's principles of life, liberty, and property, it has only been within recent years that many of these rights have been recognized in the work place. Demands for privacy. Demands for safety. Demands for education. Demands for just wages. Demands for opportunity. Demands for sharing in profits related to the value added dimension of labor. All have caused us to re-examine the meaning of the term *inalienable rights*. What do we mean by the right to life? To liberty? To the pursuit of happiness? All are examples of the rebellious spirit of individualism advanced by John Locke.

Accordingly, it is this spirit of individualism that altered the Western mind. Abolishing elitism and privilege, it brought a new perspective to the leadership dyad. No one, by nature, is superior to another. There is no divine right of kings. All of us are free to follow our passions, our desires, and our dreams. We can only be ruled by our own consent, and the social contract is the vehicle of that consent. Scoffing at the teachings of those who taught that man is a victim of fear and self-interest, Locke believed that egotism can be tempered by reason, that self-interest can be tempered by enlightenment, that cooperation can best serve the interests of all parties to an agreement. Thus, his contract for a civil society both allows for and limits the extent of mutual exploitation among people.

These ideas are Locke's gifts to Western culture. More specifically, these ideas are Locke's gift to America. Again, Robert Goldwin explains,

> John Locke has been called America's philosopher, our king in the only way a philosopher has ever been a king of a great nation. We, therefore, more than many other peoples in the world, have the duty and the experience to judge the rightness of his teaching.[13]

Indeed, it is our duty to judge the rightness of his teaching.

Notes

1.　John Locke, *Two Treatises of Civil Government* (London: J.M. Dent & Sons, Lid., 1943), 119.

2.　Ibid., 61.

3.　Ibid., 118.

4.　Ibid., 130.

5.　Ibid., 123

6.　Ibid., 183-184.

7.　Ibid., 159.

8.　Ibid., 192.

9.　Ibid., 145-147.

10.　Ibid., 156-157.

11.　Ibid., 157-158.

12.　Robert A. Goldwin, "John Locke," in Leo Strauss and Joseph Cropsey, eds., *History of Political Philosophy* 3rd. ed. (Chicago: University of Chicago Press, 1987), 510.

13.　Ibid.

7

Rousseau on Leadership:
Guiding the Wills of Men

"Oh ye people who are free, remember this maxim: Liberty may be acquired, but never recovered.*"*
—Jean-Jacques Rousseau

Cries for liberty began to swell during the last half of the eighteenth century in Western society. And, the sparks of revolution were not limited to England and the colonies of the New World. In France, Voltaire's literary attack against the ecclesiastical authority of the church had set the stage for political discontent. Inspired by these writings, Jean-Jacques Rousseau had lashed out against the French aristocracy, those who "gorge themselves with superfluities while the starving multitude are in want of the bare necessities of life." Thus, as we move across the channel toward the Continent in our attempt to gain a more complete understanding of the leadership dyad, we discover a landscape filled with turmoil. We find ideas that would provide new meaning to the terms *Liberté, Egalité,* and *Fraternité.* In brief, we enter the world of Jean-Jacques Rousseau, and whether it be in his *Discourse on the Sciences and Arts, Discourse on the Origins and Foundations of Inequality among Men, Discourse on Political Economy, Emile,* or *The Social Contract*, we find a mind filled with the relentless passion of revolt against privilege.

Moreover, we find writings renouncing philosophies that give primacy to reason, for unlike Locke or Hobbes and the rationalists who emerged from the Age of Enlightenment, Rousseau scoffed at those who taught that reason could bring understanding regarding the nature of man. Instead, he searched within man's soul, within his feelings, his desires, his instincts. Reason, he believed, had stifled humankind. It had reduced men to mere mechanistic organisms controlled by the forces of natural law. It had legitimized one man's dominance over another. It had justified inequality, providing abundance for the elite and famine for the poor. For Rousseau, not only had reason placed man in bondage, it had transformed him into a *depraved animal.*

Thus, imbedded within Rousseau's teachings are the seeds of Romanticism. As a Platonist, he argued against the rationalists. One's mind *is not* a blank slate at birth, a *tabula rasa*, to be informed by experiences acquired through the senses. Rejecting the primacy of reason, he focused on the supremacy of man's instincts and passions. If we wish to discover truth, Rousseau taught, we should not look outward with syllogistic analysis. Instead, we must look inward to the nature of our souls, for it is there that we find truth. Within our souls resides the will of God.

It is within this context, then, that Rousseau explored concepts related to the leadership dyad. Book I, Chapter I, of *The Social Contract* begins as follows:

> Man is born free, and yet we see him everywhere in chains. Those who believe themselves the masters of others cease not to be even greater slaves than the people they govern. How this happens I am ignorant; but, if I am asked what renders it justifiable, I believe it may be in my power to resolve the question.
>
> If I were only to consider force, and the effects of it, I should say, 'When a people is constrained to obey, and does obey, it does well; but as soon as it can throw off its yoke, and does throw it off, it does better: for a people may certainly use, for the recovery of their liberty, the same right that was employed to deprive them of it: it was either justifiably recovered, or unjustifiably torn from them.' But the social order is a sacred right which serves for the basis of all others. Yet this right comes not from nature; it is therefore founded on conventions.[1]

In summary, Rousseau maintained that although man is born free, he finds himself subject to the will of others. And whereas Hobbes and Locke and many of their Greek predecessors had proposed a proper social order rooted in reason and the laws of nature, Rousseau held that social order is not *natural* at all. It is a mere convention of society. It is simply an agreement among men. Thus, if we want to understand humankind, he argued, we must understand its history. It is convention, not nature, that gives rise to the leadership dyad.

First, he explained, the *natural* family cannot be the basis of civil society, for once a child reaches maturity, he is exempt from obedience to the will of his parents:

The earliest and the only natural societies are families: yet the children remain attached to the father no longer than they have need for his protection. As soon as that need ceases, the bond of nature is dissolved. The child, exempt from the obedience he owed the father, and the father, from the duties owed the child, return equally to independence. If they continue to remain together, it is not in consequence of a natural, but a voluntary union; and the family itself is maintained only by a convention.[2]

Second, he argued, force cannot be the natural foundation of society, for obedience is due only to legitimate powers. *Might making right* can never be considered a legitimate basis for authority:

If it is necessary to obey by force, there can be no occasion to obey from duty; and when force is no more, all obligation ceases with it. We see, therefore, that this word 'right' adds nothing to force, but is indeed an unmeaning term.

* * *

We must grant, therefore, that force does not constitute right, and that obedience is only due to legitimate powers.[3]

Thus, he rejected Aristotle's notion that some men are born to rule while others are born to be slaves, teaching that at birth all men are free. Aristotle, Rousseau believed, had mistakenly identified the effect of slavery as its cause. "If there are some who are slaves by nature, the reason is that men were made slaves against nature," he writes. "Force made the first slaves, and slavery, by degrading and corrupting its victims, perpetuated their bondage."[4]

One can, of course, sell oneself for subsistence. We cannot, however, legitimately renounce our liberty:

To say that a man gives himself gratuitously is absurd and incomprehensible; such an act is unjustifiable and void, because the person who performed it is not in his proper senses. To say the same of a whole people is to suppose the people are all mad; and folly does not make it right.

* * *

To renounce our liberty is to renounce our quality of man, and with it all the rights and duties of humanity. No adequate compensation can possibly be made for a sacrifice so complete. Such a renunciation is incompatible with the nature of man; whose actions, when once he is deprived of his free will, must be destitute of all morality. Finally, a convention which stipulates absolute authority on one side, and unlimited obedience on the other, must be considered as vain and contradictory.[5]

In our primitive state of nature, Rousseau explains, there was no leadership dyad. No person had the right to exact obedience from another. All lived in a state of goodness as they followed their passions and instincts, and what few needs they had were quickly and fully satisfied. Nevertheless, since not all were born with equal capacities, some were at a disadvantage regarding the acquisition of the necessities of life. Consequently, humans formed social contracts to protect their lives as well as their possessions, and it is these contracts that placed them in bondage. Rather than assure people of their freedoms, however, they bound them in chains. Carefully concocted by those claiming supernatural authority based on natural law, these social contracts allowed some to gain advantage over others. Thus, it is not nature that causes injustices among men. Rather it is society. It is convention that limits our liberties.

Certainly, Rousseau agreed that humans could not have survived in their primitive state, for the strength of individuals would not have been sufficient to overcome the obstacles of self-preservation. "This primitive state can therefore subsist no longer"; he states, "and the human race would perish unless it changed its manner of life."[6] Yet, the contract Rousseau proposed was quite different from that of Hobbes or Locke. It was not based on fear or fraud or deficiencies within nature. Rather, his social contract was based upon the sanctity of the *general will* of the community. It was based on the forfeiture of *individual* liberties in exchange for *civil* liberties. He explains,

> The articles of the social contract will, when clearly understood, be found reducible to this single point: the total alienation of each associate, and all his rights, to the whole community; for, in the first place, as every individual gives himself up entirely, the condition of every person is alike; and being so, it would not be to the interest of any one to render that condition offensive to others.
>
> Nay, more than this, the alienation being made without any reserve, the union is as complete as it can be, and no associate has any further claim to anything: for if any individual retained rights not enjoyed in general by all, as there would be no common superior to decide between him and the public, each person being in some points his own judge, would soon pretend to be so in everything; and thus would the state of nature be continued and the association necessarily become tyrannical or be annihilated.

* * *

If, therefore, we exclude from the social compact all that is not essential, we shall find it reduced to the following terms:

> *Each of us places in common his person and all his power under the supreme direction of the general will; and as one body we all receive each member as an indivisible part of the whole.*[7]

Indeed, Rousseau recognized the many implications of such a trade-off. Certainly, we lose our *natural* liberties. We are no longer free to do as we please as we follow the instincts of our nature. Nevertheless, in exchange for our *individual* liberties, we gain our *civil* liberties as we become an indivisible part of the entire community. Moreover, by accepting the justice of the *general will*, we gain a *moral* liberty that we lacked in the primitive state of nature. By *choosing* to submit our private wills to the *general will*, we are no longer subject to the primitive passions of our instincts. In brief, by relinquishing our freedom, we force ourselves to become free.

Under Rousseau's social contract, not only does one relinquish his private will to the *general will* of the community, he also foregoes his individual rights to property. Ownership, he taught, should be allocated by the *general will* of the people, for no person, he believed, should ever be wealthy enough to buy another, nor should one be so poor that he would be forced to sell himself. Thus, within his community "the right which each individual has over his own property is always subordinate to the right which the community has over all; without which there would be no solidity in the social bond, nor any real force in the exercise of sovereignty."[8]

In this manner, Rousseau believed that all citizens would be assured both liberty and equality. At the conclusion of Book I of *The Social Contract*, he explains as follows:

> I shall conclude this chapter and book with a remark which must serve for the basis of the whole social system: it is that, instead of destroying the natural equality of mankind, the fundamental compact substitutes, on the contrary, a moral and legal equality for that physical inequality which nature placed among men, and that, let men be ever so unequal in strength or in genius, they are all equalized by convention and legal right.[9]

According to Rousseau, the underlying foundation of this *legal right* resides in the *general will*. It cannot err, for it has no self-interest against any individual citizen. It is indivisible. Since it seeks to promote the common safety and well being of all citizens, it becomes the absolute measure of justice. Thus, one could always test the validity of his often self-serving private will by comparing it to the *general will*. If a discrepancy exists, the private will is in error.

The *general will*, however, should not be confused with the *will of all*. Such is an important distinction. They are not the same, for the *will of all* is only a sum of private wills, and, as such, it often contains greed and selfishness. Thus, the *will of all* might not always reveal the truths of the *general will*. The *general will*, however, is an abstract entity that pre-exists the *will of all*. It is concerned only with the common good; it is not influenced by individual interests. Within the *general will* lies the will of God.

Who, then, should lead? Does any person have a right to exact obedience from another? On the surface it would appear that under this social contract there would be no leaders. Following the directives of the *general will* toward the common good, the people would lead themselves. Yet, Rousseau's answers to these questions are far more complex than they might appear, for although he believed in the liberty and equality among humankind, he also held that some have more ability than others to decipher the truths of the *general will*.

First, he explains, *goodness* exists independently of human existence, i.e., all *justice* flows from God. It is universal. It applies to all. And, according to Rousseau, it is through the *general will* of the people that God's justice is revealed. Since it is determined *by* all people *for* all people, it cannot be advantageous to some and detrimental to others. Consequently, it is through this *general will* that laws are derived to direct God's justice toward its proper end. Thus, in this rather Utopian understanding of the nature of law, there are no leaders. All follow the *general will* of the people.

But Rousseau was not a Utopian. Although egalitarian in his compassion for the masses, he feared that their decisions might lack wisdom and understanding. Thus, even though he taught that the *general will* is always right, he also held that the judgment that guides it is not always enlightened. Leaders would be needed to help the masses understand God's justice. Rousseau explains,

> How can an unenlightened multitude, which often does not know what it wants, since it so seldom knows what is good for it, execute, of itself, so great, so difficult an enterprise as a system of legislation? Of themselves the people always will the good, but of themselves they do not always see in what it consists. The general will is always right, but the judgment that guides it is not always enlightened. It is therefore necessary to make the people see things as they are, and sometimes as they ought to appear, to point out to them the right path which they are seeking, to guard them from the seducing voice of private wills, and, helping them to see how times and places are connected, to induce them to balance the attraction of immediate and sensible advantage against the apprehension of unknown and distant evil. Individuals see the good they reject; the public wills the good it does not see. All have equally need for guidance. Some must have their wills made conformable to their reason, and others must be taught what it is they will. . . . From thence is born the necessity of a legislator.[10]

Who should lead? The people? Ultimately, yes, for it is they who participate in the *general will*. Since, however, the masses are incapable of knowing the common good, they *must have their wills made conformable* to the wills of the enlightened few.

Rousseau is rather vague, however, as to who these leaders, these enlightened few, might be. First, he proposes that as servants of the people, legislators might be elected by the people. Later, he suggests that since all are equal, selection by lots might be more appropriate in a true democracy. Although he is not clear on this issue, he is quite precise as he discusses the qualities necessary to be a legislator: "if it be true that a great prince is a rare man, how much more rare must be a good legislator?" He continues,

> Those who dare to undertake the institution of a people must feel themselves capable, as it were, of changing human nature, of transforming each individual, who by himself is a perfect and solitary whole, into a part of a much greater whole, from which he in some measure receives his being and his life; of altering the constitution of man for the purpose of strengthening it; of substituting a moral and partial existence instead of the physical and independent existence which we have all received from nature.[11]

In addition, Rousseau suggested that leaders must often point to supernatural authority as the source of their inspiration and wisdom if they are to be successful in their attempt to guide the wills of the masses. In brief, those who wish to influence the wills of others must claim that God has sanctioned their judgment:

> It is this that has, in all ages, obliged the founders of nations to have recourse to the intervention of Heaven and to attribute to the gods what has proceeded from their own wisdom, that the people might submit to the laws of the State as to those of nature and, recognizing that the same power which formed man created the city, obey freely, and contentedly endure that restraint so necessary to public happiness.
>
> This sublime reason, so far above the comprehension of vulgar men, is that whose decisions legislators put in the mouth of the immortals, that those might be led along under the sanction of divine authority, whom it might be impossible for human prudence to conduct without it.[12]

In many ways Rousseau's legislators resemble Plato's philosopher-kings. Only they know the ultimate good. Their role is to guide those less capable than themselves toward justice. Yet, whereas Plato proposed that such a hierarchy existed as a part of the natural order, Rousseau maintained an insistence on equality. Even though the leader might be superior in ability and understanding, he ultimately, like his followers, remains subject to the *general will*.

Consequently, the leader's task is to convince the follower that his ideas are their ideas, that his will is their will. In his book, *Rousseau's Social Contract*, Lester Crocker explains as follows,

> One function of the guide, or Legislator, is, then, to tell the people what they ought to think and what they want. It is he who makes the people 'sufficiently informed.' The 'educational' role of the State begins with the Legislator, and the purpose of 'education' is to prepare consent ('docility') and 'liberty' by changing wills. That the people should will consent ('of their own desire') is necessary; . . . The role of the guide is to see to it that the citizens make their own decisions as they should; that while they do as they wish, they wish what they *should* wish. . . . Rousseau is the inventor of what is now euphemistically called 'guided democracy'[13]

The successful leader, then, is one who can persuade others to align their wills to his. In this manner, the unity of the organization remains intact.

This is especially true as the *general will* relates to law and public opinion. In his discussion regarding legal relationships within the community, Rousseau explains as follows:

> To these three sorts of laws there must be united a fourth, which is the most important of all, and is not inscribed on brass or marble, but in the hearts of the citizens. This makes the true constitution of the State; its powers increase by time; and when all other laws become feeble or even extinct, this reanimates them or supplies their place. This preserves among a people the true spirit of their institution, and substitutes insensibly the force of habit for that of authority. I speak of manners and morals, customs, and more than all, of opinions; these are means unknown to our political thinkers, but on which the success of everything else depends. To them the great legislator directs his *secret* (italics added) care, though he appears to confine his attention to particular laws, which are only the curve of the arch, while manners and morals, slower to form, will become at last the immovable key-stone.[14]

Consequently, not only must the leader influence the opinions of the followers, he must do so surreptitiously. They must not know that he is *guiding* them. The illusion of the *private will* must be maintained, for without it, the follower's belief in his individual freedom would be destroyed.

Returning to Rousseau's answers to our questions regarding the leadership dyad, while on the surface it appears that leaders and followers are somewhat equal, in actuality they are not. Certainly, his thought demonstrates an intense passion for the rights of all people. He abhorred privilege. He sought freedom for all. Yet, in his attempt to provide liberty, he subjugates individual wills to the surreptitious control of the leader. As a result, the *general will* often becomes little more than the will of the most persuasive, the most cunning, and the most devious. Thus, in his attempt to elevate man from *natural liberty* to *civil liberty* to *moral liberty*, Rousseau managed to relegate him to the manipulation of a privileged few. Lester Crocker describes this relationship as follows:

> Men, unless they are remade and under continuous control, cannot be trusted to distinguish between good and evil, or not to prefer the personally useful to the socially harmful. Judgment and decision therefore belong to an elite of leaders. The people, unable to think or will correctly, are called on to obey and to believe. Because Rousseau has no confidence either in their reason or in their impulses, his whole thinking points to a system of hidden control by a few Wolmarian leaders under the guise of self-government and liberty.[15]

From this perspective, then, leaders are those who can persuade others to share with them their understanding of the common good, and while Rousseau taught that leaders serve only at the pleasure of the followers, their right to lead is ultimately based on their ability to maintain a hidden control. It is based on their ability to perpetuate an illusion of liberty and equality among men.

Although Rousseau's teachings are vague as to who among the people should lead, women would not be included among his legislators. Instead, as he delineates his education programs, he proposes that women should be treated differently than men: they should be taught to serve men and make them happy. As Professor S. E. Frost, Jr. explains, "While the boy should be free to develop according to his own inner nature, the girl should be molded to fit the pattern demanded by the man."[16] For Rousseau, however, such a pattern is not a matter of innate inferiority. Instead, it is because obedience is what society has taught her. It is convention, not *nature,* that has defined her proper role.

Such are a few of Rousseau's contributions toward our understanding of leadership. Indeed, they are complex. As a result, one might find his ideas as supportive for a number of seemingly contradictory leadership theories in Western culture. If, for example, we focus on his supposition that man, by nature, is basically good and that it is society that brings evil into his life, we can conclude that many of the behavioral scientists of the twentieth century would take solace in the teachings of Rousseau. Leaders who pay heed to motivational theories that confirm the importance of the human dimension within organizations are philosophically in harmony with his teachings.

Similarly, leaders who advocate egalitarianism within the social order share the philosophical beliefs of Rousseau, for in many ways, he laid the political foundation for the socialist democracies of Western Europe. In fact, many argue that his teachings were the seeds that would germinate into communism nearly 100 years later. In any event, leaders who share his belief that privilege and inequality must be eradicated within our societies and organizations will recognize their philosophical underpinnings in the works of Rousseau.

On the contrary, one might reasonably argue that the political philosophy of Rousseau has served to buttress totalitarian leadership in Western society, for such an autocratic leadership style is based on control. It is nurtured by surreptitious double-talk. It flourishes when leaders believe that only they have the ability to discern what is good, what is true. It thrives when the elite, whether liberal or conservative in their ideologies, are convinced that it is their task to mold the wills of the less informed masses to conform with their own. Obey and believe. Mind control. Human engineering. Conformity. Behavior modification. Whether found in the political arena, religious sanctuaries, or the corporate board room, all are concepts embedded in the philosophy of Rousseau.

Moreover, to a great extent environmentalists and communitarians, those who seek to distinguish between what is *rightly mine* and what is *rightly ours*, often share Rousseau's belief that the private wills of individuals lead to the disruption of the social order. They share his proposition that if greed and self-serving interest were allowed to rule, then the concept of *rightly ours* would hold little sway within our communities.

More important to our understanding of leadership, however, is Rousseau's proposition that human nature is transformed by history. Prior to the eighteenth century, man had viewed his nature as being constant and consistent. It would never change. Rousseau was among the first to argue that history influences the nature of humankind. It is continuously changing. Although we maintain certain primeval characteristics, he taught, it is the conventions of society that influence most heavily what we are and what we will become. And it is this proposition that is most important, for as Jean-Jacque Rousseau altered our understanding of the nature of humankind, so, too, did he alter our perspective regarding of the leadership dyad in Western culture.

Notes

1. Jean-Jacques Rousseau, *The Social Contract* (New York: Hafner Publishing Company, 1947), 5.
2. Ibid., 6.
3. Ibid., 8-9.
4. Ibid., 7.
5. Ibid., 10.
6. Ibid., 14.
7. Ibid., 15.
8. Ibid., 21-22.
9. Ibid., 22.
10. Ibid., 35.
11. Ibid., 36.
12. Ibid., 38.
13. Lester G. Crocker, *Rousseau's Social Contract* (Cleveland, OH: Case Western University Press, 1968), 74.
14. Rousseau, 49.
15. Crocker, 87.
16. S. E. Frost, Jr., *Basic Teachings of the Great Philosophers* (New York: Doubleday Anchor Books, 1962), 221.

8

Hegel on Leadership:
The Unfolding of the Absolute

"What is rational is actual, and what is actual is rational."
—Georg W. F. Hegel

From the seeds of revolution that had germinated in England and France during the last half of the eighteenth century grew political and economic upheaval. The United States had declared its independence. The concept of the crown had become tarnished. The consciousness of the French people had erupted in revolt. The Napoleonic Wars had brought havoc to the nations of Europe, and social order throughout the Continent had been threatened.

Rather than embrace concepts of liberty taking root in England, France, and the New World, however, most German philosophers had rejected the underpinnings of democracy in favor of a worldview that acknowledged the absolute power of the state. They scorned concepts of individual freedoms and inalienable rights. *Responsibility* was far more important than *freedom*; only through *duty* could one become liberated from oneself.

Unquestionably, the most prolific and influential among these philosophers during the early years of the nineteenth century was Georg W. F. Hegel. His body of work is encyclopedic; it includes writings not only in philosophy but religion, art, ethics, and history. Thus, in our quest to gain a more enriching understanding of leadership, it is imperative that we examine his thought, for not only did he depart from those who had advocated individualism within the leader-follower dyad, he demanded that our considerations expand well beyond the nature of social contracts. Not only must we grapple with concepts regarding the nature of man, we must examine these concepts within a context that embodies the totality of existence.

We begin our journey by considering Hegel's understanding of the mind of man, for the mind, he believed, was simply a microcosm of the macrocosm of all reality. Accordingly, Hegel was an Idealist. He did not believe, however, that man's knowledge is directed toward an external *Ideal*. Instead, he held that man's ideas are a part of the *Ideal* itself.

As he developed his philosophy, Hegel observed that man's knowledge is always changing. It continuously moves from a state of unawareness to a state of consciousness. It affirms what it knows. Then it discovers the opposite of what it believes to be true, and a state of inner-conflict occurs. Finally, in order to restore consonance within itself, it synthesizes these opposites into one. Professor S. E. Frost summarizes the process as follows:

> If one studies the mind, he will find it full of contradictions, full of disagreements, of opposites. But, a further study will reveal that there is a process in the mind by which each pair of opposites is reconciled in a synthesis which includes both but on a higher level.
>
> This process is everywhere. First there is a thesis or affirmation, then we discover the antithesis to this thesis or its contradiction. The highest form of thought is the reconciling of both in a synthesis which lifts thinking one step higher. The human mind does not stop with contradictions, but strives to get rid of them by effecting a synthesis. This is not to be confused with a compromise. In a true synthesis the values of both the thesis and the antithesis are conserved and together they move toward new values.
>
> The highest function of the mind, then, is that activity which enables one to see things whole, to see opposites unified. Here man rises to the true height of his nature. Thought moves from the simple ideas to more complex notions, from the individual to the rich and full.[1]

Hegel believed that the process of the mind and the process of nature are the same. As the ideas of man evolve through the dialectic process, so, too, does the *universal mind* of all reality. It begins with a thesis. It proceeds to contradiction. It resolves through synthesis. From this synthesis develops a new antithesis, and the contradiction is resolved through a new and higher synthesis, *ad infinitum*.

History, then, records the unfolding of this dialectic. Man is not separate from the *Ideal* but is a part of it. His reason participates in divine reason. As such, the mind of man and the mind of God are one. It is this Spirit, this *Geist*, that drives the evolution of the universe: "reason is the *substance* of the universe," Hegel states, "that by which and in which all reality has its being and subsistence."[2] Historian Richard Tarnas explains it this way:

The world is the history of the divine's unfolding, a constant process of becoming, an immense drama in which the universe reveals itself to itself and achieves its freedom. All struggle and evolution are resolved in the realization of the world's *telos*, its goal and purpose. In this great dialectic, all potentialities are embodied in forms of ever-increasing complexity, and all that was implicit in the original state of being gradually becomes explicit. Man–his thought, his culture, his history–is the pivot of that unfolding, the vessel of God's glory. Hence theology for Hegel was replaced by the comprehension of history: God is not beyond the creation, but is the creative process itself. Man is not the passive spectator of reality, but its active co-creator, his history the matrix of its fulfillment. The universal essence, which constitutes and permeates all things, finally comes to consciousness of itself in man. At the climax of his long evolution, man achieves possession of absolute truth and recognizes his unity with the divine spirit that has realized itself within him.[3]

Within this context we can begin to unravel Hegel's thought regarding the nature of the leadership dyad. Unlike Locke or Rousseau, he held no presuppositions regarding the inalienable rights of man. In the state of nature, Hegel notes, man is little more than an animal. He is savage. He is barbaric. Within the primitive state, man has not become aware of his consciousness, and, as a result, he cannot be free, for freedom demands that the consciousness of the will be exercised. Thus, he lives in a state of *unfreedom*. In his work, *Philosophy of History*, Hegel explains,

What we find such a state of nature to be in actual experience answers exactly to the idea of a *merely* natural condition. Freedom as the *ideal* of that which is original and natural, does not exist *as original and natural*. Rather must it be first sought out and won; and that by an incalculable medial discipline of the intellectual and moral powers. The state of nature is, therefore, predominantly that of injustice and violence, of untamed natural impulses, of inhuman deeds and feelings. Limitation is certainly produced by society and the state, but it is a limitation of the mere brute emotions and rude instincts; as also, in a more advanced stage of culture, of the premeditated self-will of caprice and passion. This kind of constraint is part of the instrumentality by which only, the consciousness of freedom and the desire for its attainment, in its true–that is, rational and ideal form– can be obtained. To the ideal of freedom, law and morality are indispensably requisite; and they are in and for themselves, universal existences, objects and aims; which are discovered only by the activity of thought, separating itself from the merely sensuous, and developing itself, in opposition thereto; and which must on the other hand, be introduced into and incorporated with the originally sensuous will, and that contrarily to its natural inclination.[4]

Freedom, then, did not exist in man's primitive state, for *ideal* freedom is that toward which reality evolves. Thus, there can be no freedom without the consciousness of the will, and as man began to evolve, he began the long process of becoming conscious of the *ideal* state of freedom. Through continuous thesis, antithesis, and synthesis, he developed law. He developed culture and religion. He gave assent to social restraint, and through his sense of responsibility and duty toward the *ideal*, he became free from the passions of his animal existence.

Yet, freedom does not come without struggle. Conflict is essential for progress to occur; it drives the dialectic. Within this context, even war can be considered good. Likewise, peace can be considered evil, for it fails to synthesize the oppositions inherent within its thesis and antithesis. "The history of the world is not the theatre of happiness," writes Hegel. "Periods of happiness are blank pages in it, for they are periods of harmony, periods when the antithesis is in abeyance."[5] Philosopher Will Durant explains the thought of Hegel regarding man's struggle for freedom as follows:

> Not that strife and evil are mere negative imaginings; they are real enough; but they are, in wisdom's perspective, stages to fulfillment and the good. Struggle is the law of growth; character is built in the storm and stress of the world; and a man reaches his full height only through compulsions, responsibilities, and suffering. Even pain has its rationale; it is a sign of life and a stimulus to reconstruction. Passion also has a place in the reason of things: 'nothing great in the world has been accomplished without passion;' and even the egoistic ambitions of a Napoleon contribute unwittingly to the development of nations. Life is not made for happiness, but for achievement. . . . History is made only in those periods in which the contradictions of reality are being resolved by growth, as the hesitations and awkwardness of youth pass into the ease and order of maturity. History is a dialectical movement, almost a series of revolutions, in which people after people, and genius after genius, become the instrument of the Absolute.[6]

Freedom, then, evolves through the conflict of history, with each stage raising man's level of consciousness. In nature, no man is free. All men are prisoners of their passions and impulses. As man's consciousness develops, he becomes aware of his own freedom; yet, he lacks the consciousness to be aware of the freedom of others. Humans continue to evolve, however, and as they meet the struggles necessary for synthesis, they become conscious of *Ideal* freedom, i.e., they become aware of the Truth that all humans, as humans, are free, and they exercise their wills to affirm the Absolute. It is only then that they become free. Hegel explains with examples from history:

> The Orientals have not attained the knowledge that spirit–man *as such*–is free; and because they do not know this, they are not free. They only know that *one is free*. But on this very account, the freedom of that *one* is only caprice; ferocity–brutal recklessness of passion, or a mildness and tameness of the desires, which is itself only an accident of nature–mere caprice like the former. That *one* is therefore only a despot; not a *free man*. The consciousness of freedom first arose among the Greeks, and therefore

they were free; but they, and the Romans likewise, knew only that *some* are free, not man as such. Even Plato and Aristotle did not know this. The Greeks, therefore, had slaves; and their whole life and the maintenance of their splendid liberty, was implicated with the institution of slavery: a fact moreover, which made that liberty on the one hand only an accidental, transient and limited growth; on the other hand, constituted it a rigorous thraldom of our common nature, of the human. The German nations, under the influence of Christianity, were the first to attain the consciousness that man, as man, is free: that it is the *freedom* of spirit which constitutes its essence.[7]

Ideal freedom, then, is not the proper domain of the particular nature of humans, but evolves only among those who become conscious of its existence.

Nevertheless, freedom requires duty. In order to be free, we must be rationally responsible. It is our duty to liberate ourselves from our passions and willingly restrain our natural impulses. In doing so we free ourselves from subjectivity and begin to participate with the Spirit, the *Geist*. "In duty," Hegel writes, "the individual acquires his substantive freedom."[8] Thus, human virtue can only be attained by our uniting our minds with the universal mind, with that of the Spirit. It is attained when we recognize the *end* which moves us to act. It is attained when we know that our own dignity is grounded in the dignity of the Spirit. And for Hegel, this Spirit culminates in the state. It resides in those laws and customs that integrate the particular interests of individuals with the universal mind. Through thesis, antithesis, and synthesis, the state has evolved to provide oneness with the *Geist*.

The *universal mind* of Hegel must not be confused with the *general will* of Rousseau. It does not represent the collective will of the people. It is in no manner dependent upon the particular wills of individuals. Rather, it is divine. It is the Absolute revealing itself to itself. Thus, Hegel scoffs at Locke and Rousseau and those who would suggest that individuals should share in the deliberations of the state. For Hegel the individual does not inform the state, the state informs the individual. In his book *Philosophy of Right*, he explains his reasoning:

> To hold that every single person should share in deliberating and deciding on political matters of general concern on the ground that all individuals are members of the state, that its concerns are their concerns, and that it is their right that what is done should be done with their knowledge and volition, is tantamount to a proposal to put the democratic element without any rational form into the organism of the state, although it is only in virtue of the possession of such a form that the state is an organism at all. . . .The concrete state is the whole, articulated into its particular groups. The member of a state

is a member of such a group, i.e. of a social class, and it is only as characterized in this objective way that he comes under consideration when we are dealing with the state....

Another presupposition of the idea that all should participate in the business of the state is that everyone is at home in this business–a ridiculous notion, however commonly we may hear it sponsored....

Since the laws and institutions of the ethical order make up the concept of freedom, they are the substance or universal essence of individuals, who are thus related to them as accidents only. Whether the individual exists or not is all one to the objective ethical order. It alone is permanent and is the power regulating the life of individuals. Thus the ethical order has been represented by mankind as eternal justice, as gods absolutely existent, in contrast with which the empty business of individuals is only a game of see-saw.[9]

As is readily apparent, Hegel had little use for democracies, for to him the evolution of the state is the *march of God in the world*. It is not a reflection of the will of the people. It is the *Ideal* as it has evolved through history. It is the Absolute. It is God.

Who, then, should lead? In whom has the Absolute posited the authority to rule? What gives one the right to exact obedience from another?

For Hegel the answer is simple. In terms of the state, a monarch should lead. More specifically, a constitutional monarchy consisting of civil servants and representatives of the various classes that constitute civil society. A monarchy provides focus. It provides unity. "This ultimate self," he writes, "in which the will of the state is concentrated is, when thus taken in abstraction, a single self and therefore is *immediate* individuality."[10] The state is saved from the risk of being drawn down into the sphere of diverse opinions. Moreover, under a monarch, leadership is always available. "This must happen," Hegel states, "since everything done and everything actual is inaugurated and brought to completion by the single decisive act of a leader."[11] He continues,

The rights of birth and inheritance constitute the basis of legitimacy, the basis of a right not purely positive but contained in the Idea.

If succession to the throne is rigidly determined, i.e. if it is heredity, then faction is obviated at a demise of the crown; this is one aspect of hereditary succession and it has long been rightly stressed as a point in its favour. [12]

In Hegel's mind the very presence of the monarch provides stability for the state, and it matters little who the monarch might be. Personal characteristics are insignificant:

Monarchy must be inherently stable and whatever else the monarch may have in addition to this power of final decision is part and parcel of his private character and should be of no consequence. . . . In a well-organized monarchy, the objective aspect belongs to law alone, and the monarch's part is merely to set to the law the subjective 'I will.'

***

Monarchs are not exactly distinguished for bodily prowess or intellectual gifts, and yet millions submit to their rule. Now to say that men allow themselves to be ruled counter to their own interests, ends, and intentions is preposterous. Men are not so stupid. It is their need, it is the inner might of the Idea, which, even against what they appear to think, constrains them to obedience and keeps them in that relation.[13]

Others, of course, are required to carry out the functions of government. Regardless of the leadership position one might hold, however, Hegel insisted that one's qualifications be based on knowledge. "Those who know ought to govern—*hoi aristoi*, not ignorance and the presumptuous conceit of 'knowing better.'"[14]

Like Plato, Hegel's held that not all men are born with equal talents and abilities. *Not all men are born to lead*:

Men are made unequal by nature, where inequality is in its element, and in civil society the right of particularity is so far from annulling this natural inequality that it produces it out of mind and raises it to an inequality of skill and resources, and even to one of moral and intellectual attainment. To oppose to this right a demand for equality is a folly of the Understanding which takes as real and rational its abstract equality and its "ought-to-be."[15]

Thus, in order to address these inequalities among men, Hegel visualized three classes of citizens. The *substantial* or immediate (agriculture) class, those who work with the soil and harvest the crops, those whose work requires little reflection and independence of the will. The reflecting or *formal* (business) class, craftsmen, manufacturers, tradesmen, and bankers. The *universal* class, civil servants whose task was to address the needs of all citizens. Similar to Plato's philosopher-kings, members of the universal class were freed from physical labor in order that they might devote themselves exclusively to the good of all citizens.

Hegel did not, however, define his classes as a caste system in which one's birth determines the boundaries of his profession. Instead, he taught that one's station in life should be determined by his natural endowments in combination with the passion of his individual will:

A man actualizes himself only in becoming something definite, i.e. something specifically particularized; this means restricting himself exclusively to one of the particular spheres of need. In this class system, the ethical frame of mind therefore is rectitude and *esprit de corps*, i.e. the disposition to make oneself a member of one of the moments of civil society by one's own act, through one's energy, industry, and skill, to maintain oneself in this position, and to fend for oneself only through this process of mediating oneself with the universal, while in this way gaining recognition both in one's own eyes and in the eyes of others.[16]

Even though Hegel structured individuals into classes, he readily acknowledged certain rights among men regardless of the class to which they might belong. All humans have the right to their own person, to their life; thus, no one should be required to be the slave of another. All have the right to choose a profession within the limitations of their individual abilities. All have the right to private property. All have the right to commerce, to enter into agreements with one another. For Hegel, however, such rights were not based on natural law as proposed by Hobbes and Locke or on convention as noted by Rousseau. Instead, they were based upon the awareness of a higher consciousness.

By the middle of the nineteenth century, however, this higher consciousness had yet to affirm an equality between men and women. Even though a Platonist, Hegel drew significant distinctions regarding their abilities:

Women are capable of education, but they are not made for activities which demand a universal faculty such as the more advanced sciences, philosophy, and certain forms of artistic production. Women may have happy ideas, taste, and elegance, but they cannot attain to the ideal. The difference between men and women is like that between animals and plants. Men correspond to animals, while women correspond to plants because their development is more placid and the principle that underlies it is the rather vague unity of feeling. When women hold the helm of government, the state is at once in jeopardy, because women regulate their actions not by the demands of universality but by arbitrary inclinations and opinions. Women are educated–who knows how?–as it were by breathing ideas, by living rather than by acquiring knowledge. The status of manhood, on the other hand, is attained only by the stress of thought and much technical exertion.[17]

In summary, then, Hegel's understanding of the leadership dyad becomes more clear. Like Plato, he believed that only the most intelligent, the *hoi aristoi,* those whose consciousness have awakened to the universal mind should assume roles of leadership. For the monarch, leadership is a right of birth; for others, it reflects a combination of natural ability and individual will. As such, Hegel's perspective concerning the dialectic of the universal mind throughout history supports the contentions of his early Greek predecessors that *leaders are born, not made.* Only he takes their proposition a step further. Not only does he recognize the talent *within* individuals that give rise to their *potential* to lead, he also acknowledges the converging forces of history that provide them the *opportunity* to lead. Will Durant explains the process as follows:

> Great men are not so much begetters, as midwives, of the future; what they bring forth is mothered by the *Zeitgeist*, the Spirit of the Age. The genius merely places another stone on the pile, as others have done; 'somehow his has the good fortune to come last, and when he places his stone the arch stands self-supported.' 'Such individuals had no consciousness of the general Idea they were unfolding; . . .but they had an insight into the requirements of the time—what was ripe for development. This was the very Truth for their age, for their world; the species next in order, so to speak, and which was already formed in the womb of time.'[18]

Without question, there are many illustrations regarding leaders who share Hegel's view of the leadership dyad. There are many who acknowledge that their roles as leaders were thrust upon them. They merely play out a role given them by destiny, by the *Geist*. For example, when discussing the rebellion in Czechoslovakia, then newly elected Czech President Vaclav Havel commented,

> The entire revolution is a peculiar drama, which no earthling could have written. It has features from all genres: it is an absurd play, it is a Greek tragedy, it is a Goldonian farce, it is a fairy tale. And I am only a second assistant to the director, or maybe one of the actors. . . . This was not my choice, it was fate. But I accept it, and try to do something for my country because I live here.[19]

Yet, Havel is but one example of how leaders within Western culture have been influenced by Hegel. When American political leaders of the nineteenth century based the annexation of Texas as well as its subsequent expansion of the United States throughout North America on *Manifest Destiny*, were they not acknowledging agreement with Hegel? When Franklin D. Roosevelt declared that his generation had a *rendezvous with destiny*, was he not basing his assertions on the teachings of Hegel?

Likewise, when leaders acknowledge that their *time has come*, are they not acknowledging a belief that somehow Providence has given them the *ability* as well as the *opportunity* to lead? Are they not recognizing the Spirit of their Age? The *Geist*? The Source that drives the universal mind? Are they not stating that regardless of the innate talents leaders might possess, without the timely emergence of situational forces they would not have become leaders? Without chaos in the Roman Catholic Church, would Luther have posted his ninety-five theses in Wittenburg? Without Hitler would Churchill have been proclaimed a hero among leaders of the free world? Without racial tension in the United States, would Martin Luther King have become a martyr for social justice? Without the historical evolution of advanced technology, would Bill Gates have emerged as the guru of contemporary capitalism? Not according to Hegel. Just as the individual mind and the universal mind are one, so too is the leader and the situation in which he finds himself. Both are interconnected parts of the unfolding of an *Absolute*.

The same is true for those leaders who believe that struggle is a painful yet necessary component of achievement, that change is necessary for progress, that man's consciousness is elevated only through the synthesis of opposition. According to Hegel there can be no progress without conflict. Satisfaction brings stagnation. Conflict, whether it be in the boardroom or the state room, is the driving force of achievement.

Equally important, the same is true for all who believe that mankind continues to inch forward toward *Ideal* freedom. Slowly, perhaps. Step by step. Conflict by conflict. Synthesis by synthesis. Whether in Yugoslavia or Pakistan, whether in Israel or Tibet, the conflict is never over. Out of every synthesis evolves a new antithesis. Always painful; yet, always forward. There is more freedom today than there was yesterday; there will be more tomorrow than there is today. Everything at any moment in time is exactly as it should be as man continues to evolve in his consciousness of *Ideal* freedom. And our leaders are the midwives of our future as they play our their roles in the unfolding of the universe.

Certainly, not all would agree with Hegel. Nevertheless, his influence regarding our understanding of leadership has been significant, for his thought would lead Western man in a direction dramatically different from those philosophers who had preceded him. His advancement of the dialectic would serve as the basis of a political philosophy that would alter the course of history in Eastern Europe. Yet, the dialectic that would follow would not be rooted in the *Geist*. Instead, it would be based on economics; its driving force would be materialism. Again, our paradigm for leadership would shift.

Notes

1. S. E. Frost, Jr., *Basic Teachings of the Great Philosophers* (New York: Doubleday Anchor Books, 1962), 258-259.
2. Georg W. F. Hegel, *The Philosophy of History*, trans. J. Sibree, as reprinted in *Great Books of the Western Mind*, Vol. 46, (Chicago: Encyclopedia Britannica, Inc., 1952), 157.
3. Richard Tarnas, *The Passion of the Western Mind* (New York: Ballantine Books, 1991), 381.
4. Hegel, 171-172.
5. Ibid., 165.
6. Will Durant, *The Story of Philosophy* (New York: Time Inc. Books Division, 1962), 277.
7. Hegel, 161.
8. Georg W. F. Hegel, *The Philosophy of Right*, trans. T. M. Knox, as reprinted in *Great Books of the Western Mind*, Vol. 46, (Chicago: Encyclopedia Britannica, Inc., 1952), 56.
9. Georg W. F. Hegel, "Philosophy of Law," in William Ebenstein and Alan O. Ebenstein, eds, *Great Political Thinkers: Plato to the Present*, 5th ed. (Fort Worth: Harcourt Brace College Publishers, 1991), 695-696.
10. Hegel, *Philosophy of Right*, 94.
11. Ibid.
12. Ibid., 95.
13. Ibid., 146.
14. Hegel, *Philosophy of History*, 368.
15. Hegel, *Philosophy of Right*, 67.
16. Ibid., 69.
17. Ibid., 134.
18. Durant, 277.
19. Richard Z. Chesnoff, "The Prisoner Who Took the Castle," *U.S. News & World Report*, February 26, 1990: 33.

9

Marx on Leadership:
Necessity Abhors a Vacuum

"Communism is the riddle of history solved, and it knows itself to be this solution."
—*Karl Marx*

By the end of the nineteenth century, democracy had continued to flourish. Concepts of *liberty*, *equality*, and *fraternity* had become entrenched throughout Europe. Even in Germany where the anti-democratic Hegelian dialectic had inspired a new stream of philosophical inquiry, reaction against the conspicuous consumption of the upper classes amidst the poverty and squalor of the masses continued to mount. To paraphrase Rousseau, no longer was the starving multitude willing to suffer the bare necessities of life while the privileged few gorged themselves with superfluities.

Indeed, democratic egalitarianism was about to emerge as a dominant force in Western culture. Yet, it would not be rooted in the Hegelian *Absolute*. It would not be couched in terms of *natural law* and *social contracts*. Instead, it would be advanced from a perspective of purely natural forces. It would develop from the proposition that without economic freedom, there can be no political freedom, for unless man controls the means of production in society, he is little more than a slave to those who do.

At the forefront of this movement in the mid-nineteenth century was Karl Marx. Along with his close friend and colleague Friedrich Engels, he became the driving force of a political philosophy that would serve as a source of inspiration for revolution throughout the world. Before examining the impact his thought might have had concerning the leadership dyad, however, it is necessary to consider the philosophical framework from which he derived his theories.

Although he was anything but an idealist, Marx was heavily influenced by the dialectic of Hegel. History, he agreed, is the underlying force of reality. For Marx, however, the historical dialectic was not the *Absolute* unfolding and revealing itself as Hegel had proposed. Marx shunned the concept of an *Absolute*, a *Zeitgeist*. There were no *a priori* Ideas from which one might deduce universal and ultimate principles. Marx supplanted the transcendental with the material. The relativity of sensual experience had replaced the discernible, ultimate, and universal principles of the universe. Accordingly, man's values, his religion, his culture, and his social order had all been determined by the continuous grind of a dialectic consisting only of natural forces and economic realities. As Will Durant describes the relationship between Marx and Hegel, "In place of the Absolute as determining history through the *Zeitgeist*, Marx offered mass movements and economic forces as the basic causes of every fundamental change, whether in the world of things or in the life of thought. Hegel, the imperial professor, had hatched the socialistic eggs."[1]

The progressive evolution of Marx's dialectical materialism, however, did not reveal itself in the conflict between and among nations as Hegel had suggested. Instead, it found its expression in the historic struggle between social classes. First, Marx proposed, humans lived in a mostly classless society as they evolved through the processes of natural selection. Gradually, however, some gained dominance over others. Kingdoms emerged. And from the struggle between the king (thesis) and his slaves (antithesis), a feudal system (synthesis) unfolded. Subsequently, from the conflict between the feudal lords (thesis) and the serfs (antithesis), capitalism (synthesis) evolved. Then, from the opposition inherent within capitalism, that is, employers (thesis) and employees (antithesis), Marx believed socialism (synthesis) would flower, and in socialism, the dialectic would find fulfillment, for in a classless society, there would be no further need for struggle. Man would have attained perfect freedom. Thus, Marx argued, it is through the struggle between classes, not nations, that dialectical materialism unfolds.

As a determinist, Marx held that the evolution of classes within society is independent of man's will. They are determined through natural and economic forces. Man does not choose the class to which he belongs; classes are determined by the economic systems in place at any given moment of history. Man's social existence determines his consciousness. The *essence* of man, Marx argues in *The German Ideology*, lies not in his spirit but in the historical context in which he finds himself:

> It shows that history does not end by being resolved into "self-consciousness" as "spirit of the spirit," but that in it at each stage there is found a material result: a sum of productive forces, a historically created relation of individuals to nature and to one another, which is handed down to each generation from its predecessor; a mass of productive forces, capital funds and conditions, which, on the other hand, is indeed modified by the new generation, but also on the other prescribes for it its conditions of life and gives it a definite development, a special character. It shows that circumstances make men just as much as men make circumstances. This sum of productive forces, capital funds and social forms of intercourse, which every individual and generation finds in existence as something given, is the real basis of what the philosophers have conceived as "substance" and "essence of man," and what they have deified and attacked: a real basis which is not in the least disturbed, in its effect and influence on the development of men, by the fact that these philosophers revolt against it as "self-consciousness" and the "Unique."[2]

Moreover, Marx held that these same economic conditions are the forces that would eventually transfer the means of production from capitalism to socialism. Thus, it is important to our understanding of leadership that we consider briefly the underlying premises upon which he constructed his argument.

First, Marx believed that the value of a product is equal to the quantity of work that has been put in to it: *The Labor Theory of Value*. As he delineated this proposition, he distinguished between a product's *use value* and its *exchange value*. Air, for example, has high *use value*; yet, in normal circumstances, it has *low exchange* value. We all need air. At the same time, since it is readily available, we are not compelled to exchange much for it. A diamond, on the other hand, has low *use value*; yet it has high *exchange value*, primarily because of the labor value added to it through its extraction and refinement. Most of us have little use for a diamond; yet, many are willing to pay a high price for it. Thus, a product's *economic value* is determined by the amount of labor that has been added to it.

Second, Marx argued that the capitalist seeks a surplus over the value or worth of a product. He seeks a profit: *The Theory of Surplus Value*. In order to maximize this profit, managers seek to employ workers at the lowest possible cost; yet, as they sell their products, capitalists do not share their profits with those who have enhanced its value through their labor. Consequently, as employees sell their labor for increasing lower wages, they sell themselves, and in doing so, they become little more than commodities of the rich. Profits, Marx believed, are extracted from the backs of the worker.

Third, with the demand for ever-increasing profits, Marx believed that the capitalist would be in constant conflict with his competition, and in order to be competitive, companies would increase their efforts to acquire inexpensive labor. Eventually, only the economically strong would survive; the remainder would be eliminated by fierce competition. Monopolies would emerge, and a *concentration of capital* would occur. With economies of scale taking precedence over the value of human labor, workers would become alienated from themselves as well as their fellow workers. The capitalist would develop a fetish toward his products, that is, products would be perceived as having greater value than the *humanness* of those who produce them. More important, the number of rich capitalists would decrease as their wealth increased. Conversely, the number of poor workers would increase while the value of their labor decreased.

Finally, as a result of this antagonism between the bourgeoisie and the proletariat, the workers would revolt against the capitalists, and because of their sheer numbers and a strong belief in the justice of their cause, they would be successful. They would take over the means of production, and the wealth of society would become the collective property of all. Thesis. Antithesis. Synthesis. With the evolution of these material forces, man's final synthesis would be a classless society. He would finally be free. Through the dialectic of history, he would have escaped his bondage, first from the king, then from the feudal lord, and then from the capitalist. At this final stage of his evolution, he would have reached his perfection. He would have attained his freedom.

Without question, the implications of Marx's political philosophy regarding leadership are immense. For as we pose the question, *Who should lead?*, we will not find answers that include concepts such as *natural law*, or *divine right*, or *philosopher-kings,* or *guardians,* or *freemen.* The same is true as we seek to define *equality* within the leadership dyad. Nowhere will we find justification for slavery or women's servitude. We will not read that *Some have been born to lead, while others have been born to follow.* What we will find, however, is that in a classless society, the term *leadership* acquires a different connotation, for within a classless society, the notion of a *dyad* loses its relevance.

As we approach the philosophy of Karl Marx as it relates to leadership, however, we must distinguish between his thought and that of those who have attempted to implement his philosophy. Vladimir Lenin, for example, was a Marxist, but he was not Marx. Nor was Joseph Stalin, nor Mao Tse-tung, nor the many others who have advanced the cause of communism in the twentieth century. Certainly, their political philosophies were deeply embedded in his teachings; yet, the brutal and totalitarian practices they employed were not set forth in the teachings of Marx.

This is not to say that he thought ruling classes would peacefully abandon their control over the economic forces of society. He did not. He was most aware of the fact that those with control over production would not readily acknowledge what he considered to be their injustices. He knew there would be conflict. He knew that the difficult road from capitalism to socialism would be pitted with pain and struggle. Yet, as Sidney Hook notes in his book *Marx and the Marxists*, Marx constantly distanced himself from those who would destroy personal liberty in the process. Hook further explains,

> Marx's temperament was Promethean; his intellectual tradition was Greek and scientific rather than medieval and literary; his ethical ideal a society "in which the free development of each is the condition for the free development of all." Ultimately the test of all institutions was the extent to which they made possible for all persons the full and free enrichment of their personalities. This belief in freedom, equality, and individual personality distinguishes Marx radically from all totalitarians who invoke his name.[3]

Freedom and *Equality*. These are the blocks upon which he constructed his philosophy. In order to understand these concepts within a Marxist society, however, we must distinguish between what he termed *individual (egoistic) man* and *species-being*, for in his work, *On the Jewish Question*, Marx explains that man's freedom can only be realized when individual man has absorbed into himself the abstract citizen:

> Human emancipation will only be complete when the real, individual man has absorbed into himself the abstract citizen; when as an individual man, in his everyday life, in his work, and in his relationships, he has become a *species-being*; and when he has recognized and organized his own powers (*forces propres*) as *social* powers so that he no longer separates this social power from himself as *political* power.[4]

Acknowledging the influence of Rousseau, Marx explained that man must transform himself, who, in isolation, is a complete but solitary whole (*individual man*) into a part of something greater (*spe-*

cies-being). Through this transformation, man would redefine his being, for man's ultimate freedom lies in the *consciousness* of his relationship to the whole. In his essay, *The Marxian Conception of Freedom*, Andrzej Walicki discusses the implications of this awareness:

> Speaking most generally, freedom for him was the triumph of subjectivity over objectivity, the liberation of man from the domination of things, both in the form of "blind" physical necessity and in the form of reified social relations. Hence freedom in this conception had two aspects: in the relation *man-nature* [italics added] it meant the maximization of power of the human species achieved through the development of productive forces; in the relation *individual-society* [italics added] it was understood as a conscious shaping by men of the social conditions of their existence, and thereby the liberation of individuals from the impersonal power of alienated, reified social forces. . . . In both cases, however, freedom was conceived as the triumph of reason over elemental forces, the subject (collective or individual) over objectivity–both the "natural" objectivity of the physical world and the "artificial" objectivity of the social world.[5]

For Marx, such freedom could only be achieved through the consciousness of the *species-being* breaking the shackles of capitalism. Driven by dialectical materialism, total freedom would be inevitable as individual freedoms were dissolved into the collective freedom of the *species-being*. It would be determined by the laws of history, by the natural forces of economics. It would be revealed through the dignity of labor. It would become manifest in the unity of working men and women throughout the world. No longer would they be the chattel of the bourgeois capitalist, for the proletariat would control the means of production within society. Interacting as one consciousness, *species-being* would control its own destiny. Walicki explains further:

> First, Marx saw "true freedom" as realizable only after the final triumph of communism. Second, he accepted individual freedom–as an element of "true freedom"–only in so far as it was compatible with his grandiose utopian vision of the full self-actualization of human essence in history. While he thought of "true freedom" as presupposing individual freedom, he persisted in seeing the species as the subject of freedom; in other words, he was concerned not so much with individual freedom as with the "liberation" of the superior capacities inherent, as he thought, in the species nature of man. In his view "true freedom" was the unhampered development of all the faculties of man as a "species being." Thus it was not "negative" in the sense of being aim-independent. It was a means for the realization of the final end of history: the creation of a new, regenerate, superior man. This man–or rather superman–of the future was to embody Marx's ideal of a "true man," as opposed to "real men," i.e. the undeveloped and degraded human individuals of the pre-socialist epochs of history (and especially of the epoch of capitalism.)[6]

Not only were all men free in this *grandiose utopian vision of the full self-actualization of human essence in history*, as the collective owners of all property, they would all share in the fruits of their labor. "From each according to his ability," Marx exclaims, "to each according to his needs!"[7]

When Marx speaks of equality, he speaks of *economic* equality. Yet, he does not suggest that wealth should be distributed equally. Instead, it should be distributed proportionate to one's needs. Political philosopher Joseph Cropsey explains this proposition as follows:

> This is a maxim fit to serve as the fundamental law among loyal, wise, and incorruptible friends, devoted to one another with an absolutely unselfish benevolence. Among such friends, not only would no individual seek his advantage at the expense of others, but the thought of doing so would never occur to him. In this sense, duty as duty would be transcended: what the mere sense of duty dictates to a man capable of selfishness would be the most spontaneous desire of a man as member of the friendly society. His duty would not appear to him as duty. Marxian society would be a society of billions of friends warmly joined in the rarest and most sensitive union of amity.[8]

Within this society of free and equal citizens joined in a sensitive union of amity, Marx contended that some had more to contribute than others. Not all individuals are born with equal ability and talent, and some would need more than others in order to make their proper contribution to society. Communism, however, would resolve these rights of inequality as it evolved into a system that would generate wealth in abundance. Marx explains this evolution in his work, *Critique of the Gotha Program*:

> But one man is superior to another physically or mentally and so supplies more labour in the same time, or can labour for a longer time; and labour, to serve as a measure, must be defined by its duration or intensity, otherwise it ceases to be a standard of measurement. This *equal* right is an unequal right for unequal labour. It recognises no class differences, because everyone is only a worker like everyone else; but it tacitly recognises unequal individual endowment and thus productivity capacity as natural privileges. *It is, therefore, a right of inequality, in its content, like every right.* . . . Thus, with an equal performance of labour, and hence an equal share in the social consumption fund, one will in fact receive more than another, one will be richer than another, and so on. To avoid all these defects, right instead of being equal would have to be unequal.

* * *

> In a higher phase of communist society, after the enslaving subordination of the individual to the division of labour, and therewith also the antithesis between mental and physical labour, has vanished; after labour has become not only a means of life but life's prime want; after the productive forces have also increased with the all-round development of the individual, and all the springs of cooperative wealth flow more abundantly–

only then can the narrow horizon of bourgeois right be crossed in its entirety and society inscribe on its banner: From each according to his ability, to each according to his needs![9]

Yet, Marx was more an economic philosopher that he was a political philosopher, and his delineation of economic equality far surpasses his explanation of political equality. Nevertheless, within the brotherhood of man Marx believed that humans, *all* humans, would reach their perfection. Like Rousseau, he believed that the goodness of man would prevail. Joseph Cropsey summarizes his vision as follows:

> His vision of life for the generality of mankind is what the ancient thinkers conceived as the highest possibility open to the wisest and the best–the mutual love of a few noble spirits, elevated above every petty desire, free from every trace of envy or worldly ambition, willingly sharing that invaluable good which does not pass away from its possessor when he bestows it upon another and which is multiplied when it is divided, that good being wisdom. . . . The perfect society is the society, then, in which philosophy as the rule of life would become indistinguishable from justice, which also is the rule of life. In the perfect society, justice would administer itself, and it would therefore be perfectly pure because untainted by the need to coerce, to punish, or to deceive. The disappearance of justice into philosophy might be said to be equivalent to the disappearance of the political in the philosophic.[10]

Within his vision of the perfect society lies the conviction that no human would be subservient to another. Accordingly, women, too, would share in this equality. In his *Economic and Philosophical Manuscripts*, Marx details the relationship between men and women. No longer would women be considered the property of men as in the society of the bourgeoisie, for, as Marx states, "The direct, natural, and necessary relation of person to person is the *relation* of *man* to *woman*." He continues,

> In this *natural* relationship of the sexes man's relation to nature is immediately his relation to man, just as his relation to man is immediately his relation to nature–his own *natural* function. In this relationship, therefore, is *sensuously manifested*, reduced to an observable *fact*, the extent to which the human essence has become nature to man, or to which nature has to him become the human essence of man. From this relationship one can therefore judge man's whole level of development. It follows from the character of this relationship how much *man* as a *species being*, as *man*, has come to be himself and to comprehend himself; the relation of man to woman is the *most natural* relation of human being to human being.[11]

Marx knew, however, that equality and freedom among all men would not come without painful struggle. Man would need to break the chains of alienation. He would need to overcome his desires for private property. Man would need to return himself to himself, and the resolution of these aspirations would be found in communism:

> *Communism* as the *positive* transcendence of *private property*, or *human self-estrangement*, and therefore as the real *appropriation of the human* essence by and for man; communism therefore as the complete return of man to himself as a *social* (i.e., human) being–a return become conscious, and accomplished within the entire wealth of previous development. This communism, as fully-developed naturalism, equals humanism, and as fully-developed humanism equals naturalism; it is the *genuine* resolution of the conflict between man and nature and between man and man–the true resolution of the strife between existence and essence, between objectification and self confirmation, between freedom and necessity, between the individual and the species. Communism is the riddle of history solved, and it knows itself to be this solution.[12]

Having reached this utopian consciousness, one might reasonably ask what need there would be for leadership, for with all living harmoniously without exploitation of one another, on what basis would one assume a position of authority over another? If all are free and equal, would the leader-follower dyad lose its meaning? Within communism's ultimate fulfillment, Marx would respond that there would be no government. There would be no state. There would be no leader-follower dyad, for all would live joyfully and peacefully, seeking only good for one another.

Until this fulfillment was attained, however, Marx acknowledged that leadership would be necessary. Leaders would be needed to guide the people. Thus, the Communist Party was born. The *Communist Manifesto* was written. Sydney Hook summarizes the leadership role of the Communist Party as follows:

> The working class cannot succeed in its historical task without a leadership to enlighten and guide it. This leadership is supplied by those socialists who have taken to heart Marx's theories....
>
> The task set for those who agree with Marx is clearly described. They are to participate in the day-by-day struggles of the working class, encourage organization of trade unions, and conduct militant struggles to improve conditions and standards of life. They are not to rest, however, with mere agitation for immediate reforms and better conditions but must press on to politicize working-class activities and show that every class struggle is a political struggle. They, however, "do not constitute themselves a special party over and against other working-class parties" but strive to unite them in a common front. Further, "they erect no sectarian principles by which to control the proletarian movement." They do not impose a "Party line" but emphasize what is to the interests of the working class as a whole. At the same time they try to draw to the side of the workers discontented elements among other oppressed sections of the population. Finally, they seek to keep working-class parties free of narrow nationalist prejudices and, in an interdependent world with interlocking economies, teach that the fundamental interests of the international working class are of primary concern.[13]

In many ways the leaders of the Communist Party as proposed by Marx would be similar to those of Rousseau. Their role would be to enlighten and guide the masses. Their function would be to assist those *who must have their wills made conformable* to the *species being*, and as William and Alan Ebenstein explain, this directive contained in the *Communist Manifesto* is what provided Lenin his justification for totalitarianism:

> Lenin's justification of dictatorship rests ultimately, like all other apologias of authoritarianism, on the profound conviction that the majority of the people is incapable of understanding and acting "correctly." Possessing the "correct" knowledge of the laws of history and society, communists have the right–and duty–to lead the masses into a new world, though the corrupting influences of the old world may make forcible leadership necessary. In Rousseauan terms, Lenin asserts that *communists*, because of their scientific analysis of society, represent the *General Will of the proletariat*, although the Wills of All in the proletariat may be ignorant or unwilling to admit it, for they can only think of their private, individual interests and advantages. The General Will of the proletariat is therefore, for Lenin, not what the majority of the proletarians actually think, but what they would think if they were familiar with the "correct" Marxian analysis of social and economic development.[14]

Leadership, then, becomes a *right* of those who possess the *correct* understanding of Marxian principles. In Orwellian terms, some are more equal than others. Not only is it their *right*, it is their *duty* to lead those who are unwilling to dissolve their individual liberties into the consciousness of the *species-being*. As a determinist, Marx held that leadership roles emerge through the natural forces of historical inevitability. In his *Letters on Historical Materialism*, his colleague Friedrich Engels explains that one's claim to leadership is driven by the forces of economic necessity:

> Men make their history themselves, but not as yet with a collective will according to a collective plan or even in a definite, delimited given society. Their aspirations clash, and for that very reason all such societies are governed by *necessity*, the complement and form of appearance of which is *accident*. The necessity which here asserts itself athwart all accident is again ultimately economic necessity. This is where the so-called great men come in for treatment. That such and such a man and precisely that man arises at a particular time in a particular country is, of course, pure chance. But cut him out and there will be a demand for a substitute, and this substitute will be found, good or bad, but in the long run he will be found. That Napoleon, just that particular Corsican, should have been the military dictator whom the French Republic, exhausted by its own warfare, had rendered necessary, was chance; but that, if a Napoleon had been lacking, another would have filled the place, is proved by the fact that the man was always found as soon as he became necessary: Caesar, Augustus, Cromwell, etc.[15]

Thus, leaders emerge through history as they are *needed*. If not *this* one, then *that* one. It matters not who the leader might be, for leadership is determined by *chance*, by *fate*, by *destiny*. Necessity abhors a vacuum. When the need develops, a leader will rise to fill the void. From this, Marx concluded, that in his classless society, there would be no leaders, for the struggle among men will have ended. *Liberty*, *equality*, and *fraternity* would have reached their ultimate fulfillment. All humans would have reached the *correct* understanding of social and economic development.

This, then, is a brief summary of the thought of Karl Marx as it relates to leadership. Since the demise of the Soviet Union, however, little attention has been given to the influences he might have had concerning our understanding of this most elusive topic. With a rather common perception that communism has proved itself to be ineffective, leaders and managers currently pay little heed to his political thought. In many parts of the Western world, his teachings are considered to be mostly irrelevant.

Nevertheless, as one examines his writings more carefully, it becomes apparent that his ideas remain an integral part of many of our managerial practices in the late twentieth century. This is especially true if we view many of his ideas as logical extensions of the teachings of Jean-Jacque Rousseau, for Marx pushed the concepts of democratic egalitarianism to their outer limits.

Accordingly, the origins of many of our more humanistic approaches to management so popular within the last few decades can be found in the writings of Karl Marx. When we speak of *participative* management, for example, we are sharing Marx's belief that humans are quite capable of leading themselves toward the achievement of organizational goals.

The same is true for managers who recognize the meaningfulness of work, for those who believe in the quality of the work place, for those who have abandoned mechanistic hierarchies in favor of more organic structures that minimize a strict division of labor. They, too, are responding to Marx's charge against the alienation of the worker. *Empowerment. Total Quality Management. Quality Circles.* All have philosophical roots in the writings of Marx.

Similarly, when political leaders enact legislation that limits the concentration of wealth within society, they are acknowledging Marx's criticism of unbridled capitalism. Likewise, when managers implement *profit sharing* for those who have added value to their products, they are responding to the influence of Marx.

The feminine movement, too, is indebted to the teachings of Marx. Even though he acknowledged a natural division of labor among women, he was committed to their equality. He recognized the dignity of their humanity. Unlike many philosophers who had preceded him, he viewed women as more than the slaves of men. Unlike the bourgeoisie, he rejected the notion that women are the private property and chattel of their masters.

Certainly, Marx was a humanist. Yet, he was also naturalistic. He was a rationalist. He was a scientist. For Marx, economic forces drive the dialectic. Thus, he would find little argument with those industrial leaders who embrace the scientific method as the appropriate means to achieve efficiency. As a naturalist he believed that science could increase the production of wealth. As a humanist he believed that wealth should be distributed in accordance with the needs of all who produced it. As a communist, he believed that the two would merge into one consciousness, a consciousness that would bring mankind its ultimate freedom.

These are but a few examples of Karl Marx's influence regarding leadership in Western culture. Yet, they are important, for they provide continuity to our understanding. They illustrate a connection between the thought of the early Greeks and that of our leaders today. A connection between the past and the present. Between the present and the future. Between a world-view acknowledging an *Absolute* as the divine force of history and one which contends that God is dead. He stands between human fulfillment and human alienation. More specifically, he stands between Hegel and Nietzsche. Accordingly, Karl Marx stands as a direct link to the philosophical nihilism of the twentieth century.

Notes

1. Will Durant, *The Story of Philosophy* (New York: Time Inc. Books Division, 1962), 278.
2. Karl Marx, "The German Ideology," in Robert C. Tucker, ed., *The Marx-Engels Reader* 2nd. ed. (New York: W. W. Norton & Company, 1978), 164-165.
3. Sidney Hook, *Marx and the Marxists* (Princeton, NJ: D. Van Nostrand Company, Inc., 1955), 16.
4. Karl Marx, "On the Jewish Question," in Robert C. Tucker, ed., *The Marx-Engels Reader* 2nd. ed. (New York: W. W. Norton & Company, 1978), 46.
5. Andrzej Walicki, "The Marxian Conception of Freedom," in Zbigniew Pelczynski and John Gray, eds., *Conceptions of Liberty in Political Philosophy* (New York: St. Martin's Press, 1984), 220.

6. Ibid., 239-240.
7. Karl Marx, "Critique of the Gotha Program," in Robert C. Tucker, ed., *The Marx-Engels Reader* 2nd. ed. (New York: W. W. Norton & Company, 1978), 531.
8. Joseph Cropsey, "Karl Marx," in Leo Strauss and Joseph Cropsey, eds., *History of Political Philosophy* 3rd. ed. (Chicago: University of Chicago Press, 1987), 822.
9. Marx, *Critique of the Gotha Program*, 530-531.
10. Cropsey, 823.
11. Karl Marx, "Economic and Philosophical Manuscripts," in Robert C. Tucker, ed., *The Marx-Engels Reader* 2nd. ed. (New York: W. W. Norton & Company, 1978), 83.
12. Ibid., 84.
13. Hook, 31-32.
14. William Ebenstein and Alan O. Ebenstein, *Great Political Thinkers: Plato to the Present*, 5th ed. (Fort Worth: Harcourt Brace College Publishers, 1991), 721.
15. Friedrich Engels, "Letters on Historical Materialism," in Robert C. Tucker, ed., *The Marx-Engels Reader* 2nd. ed. (New York: W. W. Norton & Company, 1978), 767-768.

10

Nietzsche on Leadership:
The Power of the Will

*"I do not wish to be mixed up and confused with these preachers of equality.
Men are not equal. Nor shall they become equal!"*

—*Friedrich Nietzsche*

In stark contrast to leadership theories based on democratic egalitarianism, undercurrents of nihilism were beginning to emerge in
Germany as history evolved toward the millennium of the twentieth
century. All previously accepted ideas were being challenged. *Ide-
alism. Realism. Rationalism. Romanticism.* Nothing remained sacred.
No previous attempt to understand the nature of the universe escaped attack by those philosophers who had rejected the validity of
objective truth.

Among the nihilists who would significantly alter our understanding
of leadership in the twentieth century was Friedrich Nietzsche. Abandoning all philosophies that acknowledged the existence of tran-
scendent principles as a means to explain man's position in the universe, Nietzsche insisted that man was alone. There were no unifying principles. There was no metaphysics. And whereas Marx had
removed the concept of the divine from the dialectic of history,
Nietzsche eliminated God from the equation of existence. *God is
dead*, he would proclaim, and upon that premise he would construct
much of his philosophy.

Without question, Nietzsche's denial of universal principles has
altered our understanding of the leadership dyad, for, if man stands
alone, if there are no unifying principles, then our current under-

standing of *rights*, *equality*, *justice*, and *liberty* loses its meaning. Before considering the implications of Nietzsche's thought, however, we must first examine the foundations from which his ideas regarding leadership emerged. We must review briefly his philosophy regarding the nature of man.

Unlike those Western philosophers who perceived man as a part of a whole, whether that whole be defined as *Form*, the *Ideal*, the *General Will*, the *Absolute*, or the *Species-Being*, Nietzsche thought otherwise. For Nietzsche there is no unity, nothing gives meaning to one's life. There is no good. There is no evil. There is only nature, and nature is cruel. It is not concerned with the needs and desires of humans. It cares nothing about man's values and dreams. It is totally impersonal as its floods, tornadoes, fires, earthquakes, and other disasters wreak havoc on man's struggle to survive. And no matter how much man may resist its forces, his ultimate destiny is death. There are no rewards. There is nothing to console him. Man's struggle to live is the totality of his existence. As Nietzsche explains in his work, *Twilight of the Idols*, man is not the effect of some special purpose, of some special end. Man is not the crown of creation. Instead, he lives in a non-caring universe without values. He is alone:

> What alone can be *our* doctrine? That no one *gives* man his qualities–neither God, nor society, nor his parents and ancestors, nor he himself. . . . No one is responsible for man's being there at all, for his being such-and-such, or for his being in these circumstances or in this environment. The fatality of his essence is not to be disentangled from the fatality of all that has been and will be. Man is not the effect of some special purpose, of a will, and end; nor is he the object of an attempt to attain an 'ideal of humanity' or an 'ideal of happiness' or an 'ideal of morality.' It is absurd to wish to devolve one's essence on some end or other. We have invented the concept of 'end': in reality, there is no end.[1]

Just as Nietzsche held that the will of the universe is indifferent to the desires of man, he proposed that the wills of individual men must also be free of compassion regarding the frailties of humanity. As Darwin had demonstrated in the biological sciences, only the strong survive. The same is true among men. Yet, in Nietzsche's judgment, mankind had moved toward *weakness* rather than *strength*. For more than two thousand years the natural evolution of man had been reversed. Coddled by religion and philosophies founded on universal principles, the pitiful common man with his fear and resentment toward the strong had been allowed to define *weakness* as *good* and *strength* as *evil*. With the support of Judaism and Christianity, the masses had managed to contradict the natural instincts of mankind. In his work, *The Antichrist*, Nietzsche explains,

> Christianity should not be beautified and embellished: it has waged deadly war against this higher type of man; it has placed all the basic instincts of this type under the ban; and out of these instincts it has distilled evil and the Evil One: the strong man as the typically reprehensible man, the 'reprobate.' Christianity has sided with all that is weak and base, with all failures; it has made an ideal of whatever *contradicts* the instinct of the strong life to preserve itself; it has corrupted the reason even of those strongest in spirit by teaching men to consider the supreme values of the spirit as something sinful, as something that leads into error–as temptations.[2]

Nietzsche, thus, sought to change the intellectual paradigm of Western culture. He sought to return to the philosophies of the pre-Socratic Greeks before those teachings had become contaminated by religion and concepts of an Ideal. He sought to return to those days more than two thousand years ago when strength was admired, when weakness was scorned, not so much to imitate them, but to stand at their summit before entering once more into the valley of philosophical inquiry. Having freed himself from the sentimentalities of Western culture, he sought to build a philosophy based upon the superiority of the strong and the inferiority of the weak.

At the core of his philosophy is what he considered to be the fundamental principle of the universe: The *Will to Power*. The will to be strong. The will to gain ascendance. The will to dominate and control. Nietzsche summarizes the concept in his work, *Beyond Good and Evil*:

> Here one must think profoundly to the very basis and resist all sentimental weakness: life itself is *essentially* appropriation, injury, conquest of the strange and weak, suppression, severity, obtrusion of peculiar forms, incorporation, and at the least, putting it mildest, exploitation;–but why should one for ever use precisely these words on which for ages a disparaging purpose has been stamped? Even the organisation within which, as was previously supposed, the individuals treat each other as equal–it takes place in every healthy aristocracy–must itself, if it be a living and not a dying organisation, do all that towards other bodies, which the individuals within it refrain from doing to each other: it will have to be the incarnated Will to Power, it will endeavour to grow, to gain ground, attract to itself and acquire ascendency–not owing to any morality or immorality, but because it *lives*, and because life *is* precisely Will to Power.[3]

Deeply embedded within Nietzsche's thought regarding the Will to Power is the nature of *inequality*. As Nietzsche had observed, all within the universe strives toward inequality, not equality. The strong survive; the weak perish. The same is true, he believed, for mankind. Those with a strong Will to Power must curtail the fear and resentment of the weak who cry out for equality. "I do not wish to be mixed up and confused with these preachers of equality," Nietzsche writes in *Thus Spoke Zarathustra.* "'Men are not equal.' Nor shall they become equal! What would my love of the overman be if I spoke otherwise?"[4]

The *overman* for Nietzsche is the *superman* of human existence. He is the man with a strong Will to Power who will rise above the poverty and filth of the massive herd. He is the man who recognizes the virtue of inequality. He seeks to reverse a culture that has advocated compassion and pity for the weak. Nietzsche explains further:

> *I teach you the overman.* Man is something that shall be overcome. What have you done to overcome him?
>
> All beings so far have created something beyond themselves; and do you want to be the ebb of this great flood and even go back to the beasts rather than overcome man? What is the ape to man? A laughing stock or a painful embarrassment. And man shall be just that for the overman: a laughingstock or a painful embarrassment. You have made your way from worm to man, and much in you is still worm. Once you were apes, and even now, too, man is more ape than any ape.

* * *

> Behold, I teach you the overman. The overman is the meaning of the earth. Let your will say: the overman *shall be* the meaning of the earth! I beseech you, my brothers, *remain faithful to the earth*, and do not believe those who speak to you of otherworldly hopes! Poison–mixers are they, whether they know it or not. Despisers of life are they, decaying and poisoned themselves, of whom the earth is weary: so let them go.[5]

Drawing upon his knowledge of the biological sciences, Nietzsche fully understood the importance of eugenics in the evolution of the overman. The strong breed the strong. Accordingly, he held genetic selection to be critical for human reproduction among the overmen. The strong must not yield to the passions and temptations of the weak.

At the same time, he recognized the importance of educational discipline in the proper development of this superior race. As Will Durant explains, Nietzsche believed that perfection without praise must be exacted among their youth. There must be few comforts; the body must be taught to suffer in silence; the will must be taught to obey and to command. "No libertarian nonsense!–no weakening of the physical and moral spine by independence and 'freedom!'" Durant continues,

A man so born and bred would be beyond good and evil; he would not hesitate to be *böse* if his purpose should require it; he would be fearless rather than good. 'What is good? . . . To be brave is good.' 'What is good? All that increases the feeling of power, the will to power, power itself, in man. What is bad? All that comes from weakness.' Perhaps the dominant mark of the superman will be love of danger and strife, provided they have a purpose; he will not seek safety first; he will leave happiness to the greatest number. . . .

Energy, intellect, and pride,–these make the superman. But they must be harmonized: the passions will become powers only when they are selected and unified by some great purpose which moulds a chaos of desires into the power of a personality. 'Woe to the thinker who is not the gardener but the soil of his plants!' Who is it that follows his impulses? The weakling: he lacks the power to inhibit; he is not strong enough to say No; he is a discord, a decadent. To discipline one's self–that is the highest thing. 'The man who does not wish to be merely one of the mass only needs to cease to be easy on himself.' To have a purpose for which one can be hard upon others, but above all upon one's self; to have a purpose for which one will do almost anything *except betray a friend,*–that is the final patent of nobility, the last formula of the superman.[6]

"You that are lonely today," writes Nietzsche, "you that are withdrawing, you shall one day be the people: out of you, who have chosen yourselves, there shall grow a chosen people–and out of them, the overman."[7]

Given this understanding of the overman, one has little difficulty surmising Nietzsche's view toward the leadership dyad. The weak must be subservient to the strong. The mere concept of *equality among men* is unnatural. It is ludicrous. In his work, *Thus Spake Zarathustra,* Nietzsche explains this progression of natural dominance as follows:

I pursued the living; I walked the widest and the narrowest paths that I might know its nature. With a hundredfold mirror I still caught its glance when its mouth was closed, so that its eyes might speak to me. And its eyes spoke to me.

But wherever I found the living, there I heard also the speech on obedience. Whatever lives, obeys.

And this is the second point: he who cannot obey himself is commanded. That is the nature of the living.

This, however, is the third point that I heard: that commanding is harder than obeying; and not only because he who commands must carry the burden of all who obey, and because this burden may easily crush him. . . .

Hear, then, my word, you who are wisest. Test in all seriousness whether I have crawled into the very heart of life and into the very roots of its heart.

Where I found the living, there I found will to power; and even in the will of those who serve I found the will to be master.

That the weaker should serve the stronger, to that it is persuaded by its own will, which would be master over what is weaker still: this is the one pleasure it does not want to renounce. And as the smaller yields to the greater that it may have pleasure and power over the smallest, thus even the greatest still yields, and for the sake of power risks life. That is the yielding of the greatest: it is hazard and danger and casting dice for death.[8]

At the lowest level of Nietzsche's natural hierarchy of inequality are women. "What is womanish, what derives from the servile, and especially the mob hodgepodge," he writes in *Zarathustra*. "O my brothers–these small people, *they* are the overman's greatest danger,"[9] he states. "A real man wants two things: danger and play. Therefore he wants woman as the most dangerous plaything. Man should be educated for war, and woman for the recreation of the warrior; all else is folly."[10]

Nietzsche's most blatant indictment of women, however, is noted in his work *Beyond Good and Evil* as he declares that woman is man's greatest shame, especially as she makes demands for equality with men:

> Woman wishes to be independent, and therefore she begins to enlighten men about 'women as she is'–*this* is one of the worst developments of the general *uglifying* of Europe. For what must these clumsy attempts of feminine scientificality and self-exposure bring to light! Woman has so much cause for shame; in women there is so much pedantry, superficiality, schoolmasterliness, petty presumption, unbridledness, and indiscretion concealed . . . .
>
> To be mistaken in the fundamental problem of 'man and woman,' to deny here the profoundest antagonism and the necessity for an eternally hostile tension, to dream here perhaps of equal rights, equal training, equal claims and obligations: that is a *typical* sign of shallow-mindedness; . . . On the other hand, a man who has depth of spirit as well as of desires, and has also the depth of benevolence which is capable of severity and harshness, and easily confounded with them, can only think of woman as *Orientals* do: he must conceive of her as a possession, as confinable property, as a being predestined for service and accomplishing her mission therein–he must take his stand in this matter upon the immense rationality of Asia, upon the superiority of the instinct of Asia, as the Greeks did formerly; those best heirs and scholars of Asia–who, as is well known, with their *increasing* culture and amplitude of power, from Homer to the time of Pericles, became gradually *stricter* towards woman, in short, more oriental. *How* necessary, *how* logical, even *how* humanely desirable this was, let us consider for ourselves!
>
> The weaker sex has in no previous age been treated with so much respect by men as at present–this belongs to the tendency and fundamental taste of democracy. . . . She is unlearning to *fear* man: but the woman who 'unlearns to fear' sacrifices her most womanly instincts. . . . While she thus appropriates new rights, aspires to be 'master,' and inscribes 'progress' of woman on her flags and banners, the very opposite realises itself with terrible obviousness: *woman retrogrades*.[11]

At the top of Nietzsche's hierarchy of inequality are the overmen, the supermen, those with a strong will to power. In his discussion of freedom as noted in *Twilight of the Idols*, he explains the ultimate greatness of man as follows:

For what is freedom? That one has the will to assume responsibility for oneself. That one maintains the distance which separates us. That one becomes more indifferent to difficulties, hardships, privation, even to life itself. That one is prepared to sacrifice human beings for one's cause, not excluding oneself. Freedom means that the manly instincts which delight in war and victory dominate over other instincts, for example, over those of 'pleasure.' The human being who has *become free*–and how much more the *spirit* who has become free–spits on the contemptible type of well-being dreamed of by shopkeepers, Christians, cows, females, Englishmen, and other democrats. The free man is a *warrior*.[12]

Indeed, in Nietzsche's world, only the strong are free, and in accordance with his hierarchy of inequality, it is the strong who should lead. Leadership is not a right assigned by others. It has nothing to do with social contracts as had been proposed by Hobbes, Locke, and Rousseau: "they designate themselves," Nietzsche notes in his work, *Genealogy of Morals*, "or by the most clearly visible signs of this superiority, for example, as the 'rich,' the 'possessors.'"[13] Throughout the history of evolution, the superior have dominated and exploited the inferior, and through fear and violence, they have shaped the world to their own advantage.

In his discussion of the origin of the first state, for example, he explains that it appeared as "a fearful tyranny, as an oppressive and remorseless machine, and went on working until this raw material of people and semi-animals was at last not only thoroughly kneaded and pliant but also *formed*." Nietzsche continues,

I employed the word 'state:' it is obvious what is meant–some pack of blond beasts of prey, a conqueror and master race which, organized for war and with the ability to organize, unhesitatingly lays its terrible claws upon a populace perhaps tremendously superior in numbers but still formless and nomad. That is after all how the 'state' began on earth: I think that sentimentalism which would have it begin with a 'contract' has been disposed of. He who can command, he who is by nature 'master,' he who is violent in act and bearing–what has he to do with contracts! One does not reckon with such natures; they come like fate, without reason, consideration, or pretext; they appear as lightning appears, too terrible, too sudden, too convincing, too 'different' even to be hated.[14]

With leadership based on one's Will to Power, it is understandable that Nietzsche would have little regard for democracy. Rule by the consent of the governed could only lead to mediocrity. The *have-nots* would constantly seek to take from those who *have*. The inferior would demand equality with the superior. Eventually, society would deteriorate into oblivion.

Instead, Nietzsche proposed an *order of castes* within society that would allow individual rights in accordance with individual abilities, for, as he notes in *The Antichrist*, "In every healthy society there are three types which condition each other and gravitate differently physiologically; each has its own hygiene, its own field of work, its own sense of perfection and mastery."[15]

Nietzsche's highest level within the *order of castes* would be those elite few who find their happiness where others find destruction:

> in the labyrinth, in hardness against themselves and others, in experiments; their joy is self-conquest; asceticism becomes in them nature, need, and instinct. Difficult tasks are a privilege to them; to play with burdens which crush others, a recreation. Knowledge— a form of asceticism. They are the most venerable kind of man; that does not preclude their being the most cheerful and the kindliest. They rule not because they want to but because they *are*; they are not free to be second.[16]

The second level of his *order of castes* would consist of those who are preeminently strong in muscle and temperament. He explains,

> they are the guardians of the law, those who see to order and security, the noble warriors, and above all the king as the highest formula of warrior, judge, and upholder of the law. The second are the executive arm of the most spiritual, that which is closest to them and belongs to them, that which does everything gross in the work of ruling for them–their retinue, their right hand, their best pupils.[17]

The third level would include those who excel neither in spirit or physical strength, the workers, the drones of society, those, he explains, who find happiness in mediocrity:

> A high culture is a pyramid: it can stand only on a broad base; its first presupposition is a strong and soundly consolidated mediocrity. Handicraft, trade, agriculture, *science*, the greatest part of art, the whole quintessence of *professional* activity, to sum it up, is compatible only with a mediocre amount of ability and ambition; that sort of thing would be out of place among exceptions; the instinct here required would contradict both aristocratism and anarchism. To be a public utility, a wheel, a function, for that one must be destined by nature: it is *not* society, it is the only kind of *happiness* of which the great majority are capable that makes intelligent machines of them. For the mediocre, to be mediocre is their happiness; mastery of one thing, specialization–a natural instinct.[18]

As we review this framework, it is important to understand that to Nietzsche, there was nothing unfair about this *order of castes*. To him it was "merely the sanction of a *natural order*, a natural lawfulness of the first rank, over which no arbitrariness, no 'modern idea' has any power." He explains further,

In all this, to repeat, there is nothing arbitrary, nothing contrived; whatever is *different* is contrived–contrived for the ruin of nature. The order of castes, the *order of rank*, merely formulates the highest law of life; the separation of the three types is necessary for the preservation of society, to make possible the higher and the highest types. The *inequality* of rights is the first condition for the existence of any rights at all.

***

Whom do I hate most among the rabble of today? The socialist rabble, the chandala apostles, who undermine the instinct, the pleasure, the worker's sense of satisfaction with his small existence–who make him envious, who teach him revenge. The source of wrong is never unequal rights but the claim of 'equal' rights.

What is *bad*? But I have said this already: all that is born of weakness, of envy, of *revenge*. The anarchist and the Christian have the same origin.[19]

It becomes apparent, then, that in Nietzsche's philosophy those with a strong Will to Power should rule over the masses, the herd. The elite should lead, the aristocratic few who possess the genius necessary to exact obedience from others. And, as Nietzsche explains, they do not lead because they choose to or because they want to. They lead because they *are*. They lead because they were *born* to lead. Leadership exists within their souls.

Certainly, Nietzsche is not the first to align himself with the Great Man Theory. His *great men*, however, differ from those of Plato, or Hobbes, or Hegel, for in no manner are his leaders connected to external superior forces. Their emergence is unrelated to an Ideal, or Divine Right, or the march of God in the world, or economic determinism. As he explains in *Twilight of the Idols*, such milieu theories are the theories of lunatics. For Nietzsche, great men are the end result of historical and physiological conditioning. Their leadership roles are unrelated to the age in which they live:

Great men are necessary, the age in which they appear is accidental; that they almost always become masters over their age is only because they are stronger, because they are older, because for a longer time much was gathered for them. The relationship between a genius and his age is like that between the strong and the weak, or between the old and the young: the age is relatively always much younger, thinner, more immature, less assured, more childish.

That in France today they think quite differently on this subject . . .that the milieu theory, which is truly a neurotic's theory, has become sacrosanct and almost scientific and has found adherents even among physiologists–that 'smells bad' and arouses sad reflections.[20]

As we review Nietzsche's philosophy regarding the concept of leadership it becomes readily discernible that many of his ideas represent a dramatic departure from those of the philosophers we have previously discussed. He is the first, for example, to isolate men from one another. He is the first to abandon universal principles that unify man's existence. He is the first to define *liberty* and *justice* exclusively in terms of *power* and *dominance* rather than *right* and *responsibility*. For Nietzsche, the terms *power* and *right* are synonymous.

He is not the first, however, to acknowledge an inequality among men. He is not the first to relegate the role of women to one of subservience. Although the premise from which he constructs his philosophy is markedly different from those of his predecessors, many of his conclusions bear a strong resemblance to those philosophies he sought to decry.

Consequently, leaders who contend that they were *born to lead* can identify with the writings of Nietzsche. Likewise, those who believe that women are, by nature, inferior to men can find support for their beliefs in his teachings. Both ideas have their origin in his perceptions of inequality within the nature of man.

Nietzsche's belief in genetic evolution, however, distinguishes him from Plato and Aristotle, from Augustine and Aquinas, from Hobbes and Hegel in their attempts to delineate the concept of inequality among humans. Whereas they sought to buttress their arguments within a context of metaphysical principles, Nietzsche supported his proposals within a context of eugenics. He had read his Darwin. *Survival of the fittest.* Men are unequal because of "all that time had gathered for them."

It is understandable, then, that many of his critics find the undercurrents of Nazism to be linked directly to the teachings of Nietzsche. Certainly, there is a legitimate basis for their argument. *Master race. Triumph of the Will. Superman.* All evoke similarities between the teachings of Nietzsche and the rise of the Third Reich. Further similarities can be readily found within the political movements of the late twentieth century. *Racial superiority. Ethnic cleansing.* Nevertheless, other, more sympathetic critics effectively argue that there is little in Nietzsche's writings that would indicate support for such concepts.

Such ideas, however, are not peculiar to the realm of politics. Although more obscure, similar influences may be found in the corporate world. Thus, it is not unusual to find that those who have been *well-bred* are frequently assigned to leadership positions in Western culture. As Jeffrey Pfeffer explains in his article, "The Ambiguity of Leadership," leadership positions are often filled on the basis of heredity. Consequently, in many corporate boardrooms, being of *good stock* serves as the measurement of one's ability. Glass ceilings and invisible caste structures often inhibit upward mobility. *What one can do* is often determined by *who one is. Race horses are not bred by mules.*

Certainly, there are other examples of the influence of Nietzsche within our organizations. Leaders who view the humanistic practices of modern management to be futile attempts to coddle the weak can also find support in the works of Nietzsche. *It's a dog eat dog world*, they exclaim. Concern and compassion have no place in the arena of competition. The weak are a burden to the strong; they have no claim to the trappings of the superior few. Indeed, unbridled capitalism has been constructed on this foundation. The strong should survive; the weak should perish. These are the teachings of Nietzsche. Likewise, these are the beliefs of many who lead within the corporate world of Western culture.

The same is true for leaders who define their superiority in terms of the strength of their wills. The Will to Power. The will to control and dominate. The will to gain ascendancy within their organizations. Self-reliant and self-contained, such leaders pay no heed to the contributions of others. They refuse to acknowledge a system in which they are simply a part. Highly disciplined, they are the self-made men of our society, responsible *to* no one, responsible *for* no one. They are free of compassion; they are free of concern.

Notes

1.   Friedrich Nietzsche, "Twilight of the Idols," in Walter Kaufmann, ed. and trans., *The Portable Nietzsche* (New York: Penguin Books, 1976), 500.
2.   Friedrich Nietzsche, "The Antichrist," in Walter Kaufmann, ed. and trans., *The Portable Nietzsche* (New York: Penguin Books, 1976), 571-572.
3.   Friedrich Nietzsche, "Beyond Good and Evil," S. E. Frost, ed., *Masterworks of Philosophy* (Garden City, NY: Doubleday & Company, 1946), 689.
4.   Friedrich Nietzsche, "Thus Spoke Zarathustra, in Walter Kaufmann, ed. and trans., *The Portable Nietzsche* (New York: Penguin Books, 1976), 213.
5.   Ibid., 124-125.
6.   Will Durant, *The Story of Philosophy* (New York: Time Inc. Books Division, 1962), 396-397.
7.   Nietzsche, *Thus Spoke Zarathustra*, 189.
8.   Ibid., 226-227.

9.   Ibid., 399.
10.   Ibid., 178.
11.   Nietzsche, *Beyond Good and Evil*, 684-686.
12.   Nietzsche, *Twilight of the Idols*, 542.
13.   Friedrich Nietzsche, *On the Genealogy of Morals,* trans. Walter Kaufmann and R. J. Hollingdale (New York: Vintage Books, 1989), 29.
14.   Ibid., 86.
15.   Nietzsche, *The Antichrist*, 645.
16.   Ibid., 645-646.
17.   Ibid., 646.
18.   Ibid., 646-647.
19.   Ibid., 645-647.
20.   Nietzsche, *Twilight of the Idols,* 547-548.

Index